B

BABES IN THE WOOD

A pantomime

by Chris Denys and Chris Harris

JOSEF WEINBERGER PLAYS

LONDON

BABES IN THE WOOD
First published in 2001
by Josef Weinberger Ltd
12-14 Mortimer Street, London, W1T 3JJ

ISBN 0 85676 257 1

Printed by Watkiss Studios Ltd, Biggleswade, Beds.

This Pantomime of **BABES IN THE WOOD** was first produced by the Bristol Old Vic Company at the Theatre Royal, Bristol on November 30th 2000, with the following cast:

FAIRY TWEET	Lara J West
ROBIN HOOD	Lisa Shingler
MAID MARIAN	Sarah Desmond
NUTTY NED	Patrick Miller
THE SHERIFF OF NOTTINGHAM	Mark Buffery
DICKON	Howard Coggins
CEDRIC	Jonathan Howell
NURSE NELLIE	Chris Harris
FRIAR TUCK	Howard Coggins
LITTLE JOHN/JACK FROST	Jonathan Howell
TOMMY	George Evans/Tim Wright
TILLY	Zöe Holbrook/Rebecca Whitehead
PEOPLE OF NOTTINGHAM, MERRY MEN, SCHOOL CHILDREN	Members of the Bristol Old Vic Youth Theatre The Dancers of Acrodance 2000

Directed by Elwyn Johnson
Sets Designed by Colin Winslow
Costumes Designed by Sue Mayes
Music Directed by John O'Hara
Fights and Movement Directed by Jonathan Howell
Lighting Designed by Tim Streader
Sound Designed by Jason Barnes

CHARACTERS

FAIRY TWEET
ROBIN HOOD
MAID MARIAN
NUTTY NED
THE SHERIFF OF NOTTINGHAM
DICKON
CEDRIC
TOMMY
TILLY
NURSE NELLIE OF KNOWLE
FRIAR TUCK
LITTLE JOHN

PEASANTS
SCHOOLKIDS
MERRY MEN
KNIGHTS
MEN-AT-ARMS
FLOWERS
JACK FROST
SWANS
WATER NYMPHS

SCENES

ACT ONE

Scene 1:	PROLOGUE (*Before Panto Gauze*)
Scene 2:	NOTTINGHAM MARKET – BEFORE THE CASTLE
	Transforming to:
Scene 3:	THE SCHOOLROOM
Scene 4:	AN ALLEYWAY IN THE POORER QUARTER (*Front Cloth)*
Scene 5:	THE TOURNAMENT (*in the Castle Grounds*)
Scene 6:	THE SAME ALLEYWAY (*Front Cloth*)
Scene 7:	THE BLUE (HAUNTED) CHAMBER OF THE CASTLE
	Transforming to:
Scene 8:	THE DEPTHS OF SHERWOOD FOREST

Interval

ACT TWO

Scene 1:	PROLOGUE (*Before Panto Gauze*)
Scene 2:	SHERWOOD FOREST IN WINTER
	Transforming to:
	SHERWOOD FOREST IN SPRING
Scene 3:	OUTSKIRTS OF THE FOREST (*Front Cloth*)
Scene 4:	A LAKE IN SHERWOOD FOREST
Scene 5:	THE SAME ALLEYWAY (*Front Cloth – Songsheet*)
Scene 6:	THE GREAT HALL OF THE CASTLE (*Walkdown*)

This Pantomime is intended to be "traditional" in that Robin Hood is played by a girl and the Dame by a man with appalling taste in frocks, the story is told clearly with as much action and knock-about as possible and, very importantly, it is local to the town or city in which it is performed. It's also meant to be great fun – both for the audience and for those who perform and present it.

The local references in this script relate to Bristol – where it was first produced in 2000, so please feel free to localise as necessary and desirable.

Also, the staging is as described because we were working in beautifully equipped theatres with excellent design and production departments able to give us anything we asked for. It doesn't have to be like that, of course, and can be adapted to how much – or how little – you have at your disposal.

The stage directions, groundplans and indicated lighting, sound, follow-spot and pyrotechnic cues are only intended as suggestions and not to be in any way prescriptive.

The only sort of "flash" units allowed by Fire Officers these days are ruinously expensive and we always wrote our scripts with a liberal use of these effects only to cut them back to essentials when we saw what it was going to cost.

The Music:
Pantomime audiences do like the know the tunes so we have always used either current and perennial favourites as written or taken well-known melodies and written lyrics which stand as part of the plot and move the story along.

Some of the music we have used is out of copyright (e.g: the Act One Finale is set to Carmina Burana and is clear) *but other melodies are still in copyright and you will need to pay for these if you use them through the **Performing Rights Society*** (who offer a special – and very reasonable – deal for Pantomimes).

Mostly, though, we have found that producers prefer to choose their own music to suit and show off the particular voices of their cast.

ACT ONE

Scene One

Before Panto Gauze. A FLASH. **(PyroQ.1; LXQ.1; FSQ.1)** *FAIRY TWEET appears DR. MUSIC UNDER:*

TWEET: Hello, everybody – I'm Fairy Tweet
    The Forest of Sherwood is my beat
    But I've strayed from the glade – flown through snow and
                  sleet
    To the NICEST people you'll ever meet . . .

    (Lights up behind the Gauze (LXQ.2) to show:)

Scene Two

Nottingham Market. Outside the castle – in the snow. The characters are all skipping about in the snow and being nice to each other. ROBIN is shooting apples off kids' heads and giving them the halves. NED is chopping wood and giving it to the poor. The SHERIFF (looking very like Richard III) is playing ring o' roses with the BABES – then TOMMY jumps onto his back and TILLY whips him with a toy whip – he laughs and skips about. MARION is playing with other children, a MERRY MAN is drinking with CEDRIC. A RED-HAIRED, BEARDED BEGGAR in rags is being given alms by other VILLAGERS. A pair of SKATERS glide about – all very Brueghel and jolly.

TWEET: 'Tis Nottingham City
    In olden times
    Where the folks are witty
    And speak in rhymes

    (DICKON picks an old lady's pocket then taps her on the shoulder and gives the purse back.)

TWEET: And even the robbers commit no crimes
    And everyone is . . . NICE.

    (The Gauze Flies out.) **(FlyQ.1; LXQ.3)**

TWEET: There's Robin Hood –
    The outlaw good –

    (ROBIN robs a rich person and gives the money to the BEGGAR.)

TWEET: And Marian the Maid – of Royal blood –
            And see – here's Neddy – who chops the wood
            He's especially NICE!

            (*NEDDY smiles especially nicely and gives a sack of wood
            to a PEASANT.*)

TWEET: The peasants are pleasant lads and girls
            With flashing eyes and teeth like pearls
            But, of all the nobs and plebs and churls
            Of the Nottingham streets,
            There's none so loved by all who spot him –
            Every virtue and charm, you'll find he's got 'em –
            He's the Sheriff of Nottingham, Sir Eustace Bottom –
            He's ever so sweet!

ALL: What a nice man!

            (*The SHERIFF smiles sweetly and skips and plays tag with
            the BABES.*)

TWEET: See him frolicking in the snow –
            They're his nephew and his neice, you know –
            Their Daddy went off to fight the foe
            And never came back.
            But the Sheriff took them into his care –
            He's a second father to them I swear –
            A perfect pal for the pretty pair –
            And they nothing lack.

            (*The SHERIFF lurches through the crowd, waving, smiling
            and shaking hands.*)

ALL: (*Sing*) FOR HE'S A JOLLY GOOD FELLOW . . . !

TWEET: Folks sing as he goes his ways
            For there's nothing told in
            Town but golden
            Praise
            For the nicest Uncle of olden days.
            So . . .

            Song: HAVING A WONDERFUL TIME (ALL)

TWEET: WHENEVER YOU FEEL OUT OF SORTS
            YOUR FRIENDS WILL ALL SUGGEST A DAY IN BED
            OR WEEKEND BY THE SEA.

BUT WE THINK THAT PREVENTION IS THE CURE THAT
WORKS THE BEST
SO WHY NOT TRY OUR EASY REMEDY?

(LXQ.4; FSQ.2)

ALL: HAVING A WONDERFUL TIME!
 THERE'S NO CONCEALING THAT WE'RE FEELING
         SUBLIME –
 THE WORLD'S OUR OYSTER AND WE HAVEN'T A CARE –
 THERE MUST BE CHAMPAGNE IN THE AIR.
 HAVING A WONDERFUL TIME
 IS NATURE'S MED'CINE WHEN YOU'RE IN A DECLINE.
 DON'T LET YOUR WORRIES DRIVES YOU HOME TO
         YOUR BED
 GET OUT AND PAINT THE TOWN INSTEAD.
 JOIN IN THE FUN
 DON'T WAIT TO CELEBRATE OUR TALE HAS BEGUN
 IF YOU CAN LAUGH AT LIFE, THE BATTLE IS WON
 AND YOU'LL BE LAUGHING IN THE SUN.
 LET'S THROW A PARTY TODAY.
 FORGET YOUR HEAD AND LET YOUR HEART HAVE ITS
         WAY –
 FOR JACK'S A DULL BOY WITH ALL WORK AND NO
         PLAY.
 SO JUST RELAX AND YOU'LL FEEL FINE –
 HAVING A WONDERFUL TIME!

(LXQ.5; FSQ.1A and 2A)

SHERIFF: *(Lurking DL)* Now is the Winter and I'm overspent –
 And times is awful hard.
 I'm in arears
 For years and years
 And they made me cut up my credit card.
 Oh woe is me,
 No glee I see –
 I'm facin' utter ruin.
 So, though I smile,
 I'll be vile a while
 And plot some evil doin'.
 Me castle tumbles,
 Me stomach rumbles,
 I've mortgaged all me leases
 Yet, while I slog,
 Those little sprogs
 Are rich as flamin' Croesus!

NED: Sheriff, Tom would like a Mars bar and Tilly wants a pot-
            noodle – Should I pop to the shop and take them?

SHERIFF: (*Furious, to us*) A pot-noodle?   A Mars bar?
            I'm not made o' money!   They go too far!
            (*Aloud – Jolly.*)   Dearest Neddy – noble youth –
            Ever ready – and that's the truth
            To spoil the babes with sticky sweets,
            Pot-noodles and lots of other treats . . .

NED: Was that a yes?

SHERIFF: Of course. Of course.   Be off now – hop it.
            Buy whatever they want. (*Through gritted teeth.*)
            The little moppets!

NED: (*To the AUDIENCE*)   What a nice man!

SHERIFF: But very soon they're going to cop it.   It's time that I began.
            Twixt you and me –
            If you'll agree –
            To say not a word to the Fairy,
            I'll tell ye the lot
            Of my evil plot –
            It's brilliant, bad and scary.
            Those kids are heir
            To a fortune rare –
            And I'm the next in line
            And, with the decease
            Of my nephew and neice,
            Their fortune will be mine.
            There's only one man
            Who could foil my plan
            And that's that Robin Hood.
            So I'll force the knave
            To misbehave
            And imprison him – for good!
            (*Furtive.*)   Yet in all my wickedness, I must be wary –
            So – not a word to the flamin' Fairy!

TWEET: Dear Sir Eustace . . . (*To DICKON.*)
            Pray introduce us.

DICKON: 'S the Sheriff o' Nottin'm innit?

TWEET: Just to say
            That I'd love to stay
            But I must be gone in a minute.

What a happy place
You keep, your Grace –
I'll give credit where I can.

SHERIFF: (*Bowing, charming*) You're far too sweet,
Dear Fairy Tweet . . .

TWEET: (*To the AUDIENCE*) What a very – very nice man!

(*Beaming happily, she flies off.*)

SHERIFF: The Fairy's flit –
So this is it!
(*To the ROBBERS*) Get Robin! Don't dare to fail.

DICKON: We'll place the pest . . .

CEDRIC: Under arrest . . .

BOTH: And dump him right in jail!

SHERIFF: See that you do –
But, for now, adieu –
And don't you miss your chances.
They'll sing a song
Before too long –
You can catch him while he dances.
(*To the AUDIENCE.*) So be kind to the Sheriff, folks – slip
us a shillin' –
And spare a thought for the poor old villain!

AUDIENCE: NO!

SHERIFF: Well . . . bubbles to the lot o' ye then! (*He lurches off.*)

(*DICKON and CEDRIC go to lurk close to ROBIN. NEDDY
hobbles.*)

ROBIN: Neddy, why are you limping like that?

NED: These shoes hurt.

MARIAN: You've got them on the wrong feet.

NED: These're the only feet I've got.

ROBIN: (*Slapping thigh*) Oh, Neddy. Don't you just love the
winter?

NED: No – leaves me cold. But I did just see a snowman with a suntan . . .

MARIAN: A snowman with a suntan?

NED: Yeh – a puddle. (*Shivers.*)

ROBIN: You should wrap up warm – (*Indicating CEDRIC and DICKON.*) like these two . . . gentlemen.

CEDRIC: Yeh. It took three sheep to make this sweater.

NED: I didn't know sheep could knit. (*To the AUDIENCE.*) They get worse.

MARIAN: Oh, Neddy, you're so . . . silly!

NED: I'm cleverer than I look. I invented something so people could walk through solid walls.

MARIAN: What d'you call it?

NED: A door. (*To the AUDIENCE.*) I told you . . .

ROBIN: Enough of this . . .

NED: Yeh, that's quite enough of this . . .

ROBIN: I must leave you, Marian . . .

MARIAN: Oh, Robin, must you go?

ROBIN: Yes, dearest. There are wrongs to right, evil to fight, the rich to rob and the poor to care for . . . But, before I go . . .

             (*DICKON and CEDRIC make a grab for him but miss as he steps forward for:*)

(LXQ.6; FSQ.3)

             Music: ROBIN AND MARIAN DUET (*Romantic – whatever is popular and suitable for the voices*)

(LXQ.7; FSQ.3A)

(At the end of which CEDRIC goes to ROBIN and deliberately bumps into him and then falls over clutching his arm.)

CEDRIC: Oh! Oh! He broke me arm! He broke me arm!

DICKON: *(Seizing ROBIN)* Just a minute, sunshine, I saw that.

ROBIN: What?

DICKON: You assaulted this poor little boy.

CEDRIC: *(Springing up and grabbing ROBIN'S other arm)* Yeh. We'll have to lock you up.

ROBIN: What's the charge?

DICKON: No charge – it's free. Free – get it? He he he he . . .

ROBIN: *(Breaking away)* Alright. Enough of this. You've had your fun . . .

DICKON: Oh no . . . *(He goes to a tree and breaks off a branch to use as a club.)* The fun's just beginning . . .

FIGHT MUSIC. (LXQ.8)

(There is a quarterstaff fight. ROBIN, triumphant, shins up a creeper on the castle wall.)

ROBIN: I'd love to stay and play with you lads – but I've too much to do in Sherwood Forest . . .

(He swings across the stage and off.)

DICKON/: *(Pursuing)* Come back. Come back . . .
CEDRIC:

MARIAN: But . . . Robin . . .

NED: Don't worry, Marian. Nobody could ever catch Robin . . .

MARIAN: But who are those men?

NED: Oh, just two vagabonds who the Sheriff's taken on as odd-job men. He felt sorry for them. *(To the AUDIENCE.)* You know what a nice men he is.

AUDIENCE: He isn't . . . No he's not, etc.

NED: Oh yes he is.

AUDIENCE: Oh no he isn't.

NED: Well anyway, those two will soon learn that nobody messes with Robin Hood.

MARIAN: (*Pointing off*) But who's this coming over the hill?

NED: Yes, she looks well over the hill.

MARIAN: It must be the new Nurse – Nurse Nellie of Knowle – or whatever her name is – come to look after you two.

BABES: We don't need a nurse.

NED: She's going to be the new school teacher.

BABES: We don't like school teachers!

PEASANTS: Neither do we!

BABES: We're off.

ALL: So are we.

NED: And me!

(LXQ.9; FSQ.4)

> (*They all rush off as NURSE NELLIE enters at speed, apparently on a motorised throne with beautiful legs crossed in front and surrounded by gadgets. The beautiful legs open and she steps through.*)

NELLIE: Hello, you tinkers. I'm Nurse Nellie. That's Nellie as in . . . ?

AUDIENCE: Smelly, belly, jelly, welly, etc.

NELLIE: Alright, alright – that's enough of that. So this is Nottingham City – looks like Kingswood – more's the pity! Now, I'm the new nurse and schoolmarm at Nottingham Castle County Primary School so, when I say "Good morning, boys and girls", I want you all to say "Good morning, Nurse Nellie" Now – Good morning, boys and girls.

AUDIENCE: Good morning, Nurse Nellie . . .

NELLIE: Oh, I love children. I had sixteen of my own. The trouble
              was I had this faulty hearing aid and my husband – Jonquil
              – would say to me "Do you want to go to sleep or what?"
              And I'd say "What?" And that's how I got sixteen children.
              Right. Now sit up. Hands on heads. Heads on necks.
              Necks on shoulders . . . Oh never mind . . . I'm very tough
              on discipline and I like good manners. I like people who eat
              chips with their gloves on – like what they do in Clifton. I
              like people who wipe their noses on a hanky and not on
              their sleeve – and I particularly like dog owners who clear
              up their doggy doos. In fact, I have to say this show's
              more of an education than a panto. When you get home
              you'll say "Well, that's taught me a lesson."

              (*The Phone chirrups.*) *(SQ.1)*

NELLIE: Excuse me. It's my mobile. Hello? What's that? Is there
              anyone here called Elsie?   She's a very smart dresser?
              And she's Welsh?   A very smart Welsh Dresser? Has
              anybody seen a tall ugly thing with big drawers? Let's
              have a look . . . Yes – that's her.

              (*She hangs up.*)

NELLIE: Now, the greenbelt round the Castle is a great achievement
              and we need to build on it.   More schools is what we need.
              As Mr Blurr said: "Education, education and education.
              You agree with that, don't you, boys and girls?

AUDIENCE: Nooooo!

              (*The Phone chirrups.*) *(SQ.2)*

NELLIE: Excuse me – it's my mobile. Hello? Yes. Oh it's the
              police.   Is there anyone here with the registration number
              V234THYYJNMFDSESW1?

PLANT: Yes.

NELLIE: Well, could you move it? Your number plate is blocking the
              street.

              (*The Phone chirrups.*) *(SQ.3)*

NELLIE: Excuse me – it's my mobile. Hello? (*Pause.*) It certainly is.
                Some twit said it's a long distance from Perth, Australia.
                Well, course it is, isn't it? Stupid man!

                (*The Phone chirrups.*) *(SQ.4)*

NELLIE: Hello? What's that? Don't forget to give away the
                sweets? Of course I won't forget to give away the sweets.
                Though they don't look to me like sweet-eating people.
                Would you like some sweets? (*To phone.*) Sorry, wrong
                number. (*She gives away the sweets – or whatever.*)
                That's all there is.   But never mind because . . .

(LXQ.10)

                Song: DAME SONG (*WITH PEASANTS/SCHOOLKIDS*)
                (*Topical song of the day – whatever is the current
                children's favourite.*)

(LXQ.11; FSQ.4A)

                (*They all exit R at the end as the SHERIFF enters DL.*)

SHERIFF: (*To the AUDIENCE, shivering*)   The snow is deep – the
                wind is chillin' –
                So spare a thought for the poor old villain!

                (*MARIAN is crossing the square and hides to listen.*)

SHERIFF: Me plan is plotted – it's rather good
                I'll take the little ones to the wood
                And there I'll tie 'em up and cheat 'em
                And leave 'em for the wolves to eat 'em. *(SQ.5)*
                Then I'll be rich!   With jewels aglister!
                Once I've got rid of that lad and his sister!

                (*MARIAN gasps and hurries off. Cackling, the SHERIFF
                nails up a notice. "WANTED – DEAD OR ALIVE – ROBIN
                HOOD – OUTLAW – 1000 GUINEAS REWARD ".*)

NED: Just a minute, Sheriff . . .

SHERIFF: What do you want?

NED: Robin's not an outlaw.

SHERIFF: He is now.

NED: You can't do this to Robin . . .

SHERIFF: Who says?

NED: I do.

SHERIFF: (*Menacing*) Who says?

NED: Well, I think I heard somebody say it. I'm not sure who it was . . . (*To the AUDIENCE.*) And I thought he was such a nice man.

AUDIENCE: NO!

NED: But, Sheriff, I thought that you and Robin were friends.

SHERIFF: Not any more. Him and his Merry Men – a crowd of criminals. He's been robbing the rich and giving to the poor . . .

NED: What's wrong with that?

SHERIFF: He hasn't been giving to me! If he so much as sets foot out of the forest – or shows his nose in Nottingham – I'll have him cracked on the rack, boiled in oil, baked at the stake and battered on the battlements.

NED: Sounds like Delia Smith.

SHERIFF: And – if you know what's good for you, you'll help me to capture him.

NED: I can't do that.

(*NURSE NELLIE enters.*)

SHERIFF: But soft! Who is it that comes here?

NED: That's the new Nursie – just been for a beer.

NELLIE: (*Burps*) Pardon.

SHERIFF: Ah ha!

NELLIE: (*To the AUDIENCE*) Was that you?

SHERIFF: You must be Nurse Nellie – the new schoolteacher.

NELLIE: I is – and you are?

SHERIFF: The Sheriff of Nottingham – Sir Eustace Wilton-Bottom . . .

NELLIE: Not one of the Cotham Bottoms?

SHERIFF: No. One of the Filton Wiltons. But, Nurse Nellie – you're
            so much younger than the photograph they sent me from
            the Rent-a-Relic Nursing Agency . . .

NELLIE: (*To the AUDIENCE*) What a nice man . . .

SHERIFF: And so much – much more . . . beautiful . . .

NELLIE: What a very nice man.

SHERIFF: (*Producing letters*) And you have such wonderful . . .
            references . . .

NELLIE: (*Snatching them*) I know. It's the way I walk. I wrote
            them myself only this morning . . .

SHERIFF: Welcome to Nottingham Castle, Nurse Nellie. We hope you
            will be very happy here – coming as you do from the rural
            rusticity of Cannon's Marsh. Allow me to introduce your
            young charges. Tommy, lad? Tilly, my treasure? Come
            here, you little dears and say hello . . . Say hello to the nice
            new nursie.

NELLIE: Hello Tommy and Tilly.

TOMMY: Hello Nurse Nellie.

TILLY: Hello Nurse Nellie.

NELLIE: I'm sure we'll get on like a house on fire.

SHERIFF: (*Aside*) Until I put them out. (*Aloud.*) I'm sure you will.
            Aren't you lucky children?

            (*They back away.*)

SHERIFF: What's the matter with you? Lost your tongue?

TOMMY: My sister's feeling homesick.

SHERIFF: Homesick? This is her home.

TOMMY: And she's sick of it.

NED: She's upset about what you're doing to Robin – making him an outlaw.

TILLY: Marian's upset about what you're doing to Robin, too.

NED: All of Nottingham's upset about what you're doing to Robin. You can't do this.

SHERIFF: Oh yes I can.

ALL: Oh no you can't.

SHERIFF: I'm the sheriff of this here town and what I say – goes. (*Drawing NURSE NELLIE aside.*) This ... Robin Hood they're so upset about, Nurse Nellie ... a thoroughly bad influence for impressionable youngsters. Now. Here are their certificates ...

NELLIE: It says here that they've been vaccinated, innoculated, galvanised, simonized and passed as first class matter.

SHERIFF: Correct.

NELLIE: Also certificates for dry rot, wet rot, sticky snot, what not and woodworm ...

SHERIFF: Correct.

NELLIE: Anything else I should know?

SHERIFF: Just that ... they're such sweet children. I adore them – I just can't do enough for them – but I intend to – do for them, that is. I have a big surprise in store for them. (*Drawing her aside.*) A surprise which you must help me to spring.

NELLIE: Oh, I love surprises.

SHERIFF: Then you'll help me?

NELLIE: Is it a nice surprise?

SHERIFF: Oh yes. Very nice – (*Aside.*) For me. (*To her.*) Do you understand? Eh? Eh?

NELLIE: No.

SHERIFF: I'll explain later.   Right.   Off you all go.   Off to school!
                (*To NEDDY.*)   What have you got in that bag?

NED: (*Producing a teddy bear and giving it to TILLY*)   Just the
                bear essentials. (*To the AUDIENCE.*)   I told you . . .

SHERIFF: (*Going, cackling evilly*)   Heh heh heh heh heh!

NED: I didn't think it was that funny.

NELLIE: Now come along Tommy and Tilly.   Here, Tilly, you can
                ring the bell to let all the others know it's time for school.

                (*TILLY rings the bell, others run on for:*)

(LXQ.12;   FlyQ.2)

                Song: GOING TO SCHOOL (*To "Round the Marble Arch"*)
                (*NURSE, NEDDY, BABES, CEDRIC, BOYS and GIRLS*)

ALL: WE'RE OFF TO BLOOMIN' SCHOOL,
                IT'S BLOOMIN' SCHOOL AGAIN.
                WE WORK ALL DAY TILL WE'RE TIRED OUT –
                THERE'S HOMEWORK TO DO TO MAKE YOU SHOUT!
                WE'RE OFF TO BLOOMIN' SCHOOL,
                IT'S BLOOMIN' SCHOOL AGAIN.
                NURSE NELLIE FROM KNOWLE IS OUR TEACHER THERE –
                SHE'S REALLY STRICT BUT SHE'S USUALLY FAIR.
                WE'RE OFF TO BLOOMIN' SCHOOL,
                IT'S BLOOMIN SCHOOL AGAIN –
                YOU COME HOME KNACKERED AND YOU GO TO BED
                IT'S BLOOMIN' SCHOOL AGAIN.

                (*During which, the Set TRANSFORMS TO:*)

(LXQ.13)

                              Scene Three

*The Schoolroom. Door LC, back wall with school drawings and pictures
including Van Gogh sunflowers, blackboard LC and an open window in
the wall right.   Benches for the PUPILS.   One bench has legs at one end
and the other legs just past centre.   If one person sits on the unsupported
end and the other two get up, it tilts.*

PUPILS: Good morning to you!

NELLIE:	Good morning to you!
PUPILS:	Good morning, dear Teacher –
NELLIE:	Good morning to you!
NED:	Good morning, Nurse Nellie. She's got a fat . . .
NELLIE:	Silence! Alright alright, that's enough of that. Now – pay attention. You all make far too much noise. D'you know, when I was born, I didn't talk for a year and a half. We are going to concentrate today upon the four r's . . .
NED:	Don't you mean the three r's, Miss?
NELLIE:	No – reading 'riting, 'rithmetic and rubbish – you have to watch your r's in this business. Today we shall do handwriting. Neddy – let me see your work.
NED:	(*Giving her his exercise book*) Here, Nurse Nellie.
NELLIE:	Are you sure your sister didn't do some of this?
NED:	No, Miss she did all of it.
	(*DICKON Enters.*)
NELLIE:	You're late. You should have been here at nine o'clock.
DICKON:	Why? What happened then?
NELLIE:	Sit down. (*Looking at Ned's exercise book.*) This is terrible. What's the matter with your grammar?
NED:	She's ill.
NELLIE:	Who is?
NED:	My Grandma.
NELLIE:	I said grammar – I am – thou art – That sort of thing.
	(*NED hits DICKON.*)
NELLIE:	Why are you hitting that nice little boy?
NED:	He said some nasty things about you – said you hadn't got the brains of a donkey.

NELLIE:	And what did you say?
NED:	I stuck up for you. I said you had.
NELLIE:	Right that's quite enough of that. Neddy. Sit there.

(NED sits.   DICKON gets up.   NED slides to the floor. NELLIE never sees the bench business.)

NELLIE:	Now remember, children – life is all about education, education, education.

(Music: All stand and sing as an anthem – to "Hallelujah Chorus")
EDUCATION! EDUCATION!
(Then to "Rule, Britannia") EDUCATION!
WORK HARD WHILE YOU'RE AT SCHOOL
DO YOUR BEST AND YOU WILL FIND IT CAN BE COOL!

NELLIE:	So let's have some general knowledge – a quiz if you like – and the winner will get a year's supply of Marmite. One jar. Question: what are the inhabitants of Malta called?
TOM:	Maltesers.
NELLIE:	How do you make a Maltese cross?
TILLY:	Stamp on his foot.
NELLIE:	How do you make a Venetian blind?
TOM:	Poke a finger in his eye.
NELLIE:	That's not very nice. Behave, Tommy. What are semi-colons?
TILLY:	Commas with knobs on.
NELLIE:	I'm wasting my time. Freda – who was Noah's wife?
KID:	Joan of Ark.
NELLIE:	Where are elephants found?
TOM:	Being that size, I shouldn't think they're lost very often.
NELLIE:	What do we get from Germany?

KID: Germs?

NELLIE: Now English. Dickon, use the words defense, defeat and
            detail in a sentence.   You may confer . . . But don't phone a
            friend. Well?

DICKON: De dog jumped over de fence and de feet went over de tail.

NELLIE: De pressing. Go and sit over there . . .

            (*NED moves to the other end of the bench.   DICKON sits.
            NED gets up. DICKON slides to the floor.*)

NELLIE: Neddy – I hope I didn't see you copying.

NED: So do I, Miss.

NELLIE: Now poetry. By John Donne –
            There was an old woman
            Who lived in a shoe –
            She had no children –
            She knew what to do.
            Now, Neddy – let's hear your poem.

NED: Aunty Mary's
            Got a canary
            Up the leg of her drawers . .

NELLIE: That's enough of that.   Sit over there.

            (*DICKON has moved.   NED sits.   DICKON gets up.   NED
            slides to the floor.*)

NELLIE: Now what are the duties of a gardener?

CEDRIC: Miss, miss, miss . . .

NELLIE: Yes?

CEDRIC: A gardener is a man who goes among the cabbages and
            peas . . .

NED: Ours doesn't – he goes among the lettuces and leeks . . .

            (*All the KIDS laugh.*)

NELLIE: Silence, all of you – hands on heads.   Cedric – go and sit
             over there . . .

             (*CEDRIC sits. NED and DICKON get up. CEDRIC slides to
             the floor. Another KID enters.*)

NELLIE: You're late.   Hang up your cap.

             (*He hangs it on the blackboard. It falls to the floor.*)

NELLIE: Honestly!   (*Drawing a hook, hangs up the cap.*)   What's
             your name?

KID: Entwistle, Miss.

NELLIE: Where do you live?

KID: With me brother, Miss.

NELLIE: But where does your brother live?

KID: With me, Miss.

NELLIE: Yes but where?

KID: With me Mum, Miss.

NELLIE: And where is your brother now?

KID: He's poorly, Miss.   Me Mum sent a note.

NELLIE: Let me see . . . "Dear Teacher, My little boy hasn't come to
             school because he hasn't been.   I've given him something
             to make him go and when he's been he'll come.   Signed –
             me Mum.

NED: Please Miss, can I go to the toilet?

NELLIE: No you can't.   Stay behind after and fill the inkwells.   You,
             young man, what's your name?

KID: Wye.

NELLIE: Why?   Because I asked you – that's why.   Now what is it?

KID: Wye.

NELLIE: When you open a school you have this big book called a
               register and you have to put all the names in it.   So –
               what's your name?

KID: Wye.

NELLIE: Because I want to put it in the book.

KID: Well, put it in the book.

NELLIE: I will when I know it.

KID: But you do know it.

NELLIE: No I don't.

KID: Well you ought to.

NELLIE: Why?

KID: That's it.

NELLIE: I give up.   Now, painting.   This beautiful picture – who
               painted it?

NED: Vincent van Gogh, Miss.

NELLIE: Wrong – Hertz van Rental.   You – what does your Daddy
               do?

CEDRIC: He's in oil in a very small way.

NELLIE: What d'you mean?

CEDRIC: He's a sardine.

NELLIE: This child is a juvenile detergent.   Go and sit over there.

               (*CEDRIC sits.   NED and DICKON get up.   CEDRIC slides to
               the floor.*)

NELLIE: Ned – answer this: Napoleon conquered Egypt, he
               conquered Germany, he conquered Spain, he conquered
               Italy.   Why did he stop?

NED: He ran out of conkers.   By the way, Miss – did you know
               that the most intelligent person in the world is going deaf?

NELLIE: Oh? Who's that?

NED: Pardon? Get it? Pardon? It's me.

               (*A PIGEON flies into the classroom through the window
               (down a wire) and lands on the teacher's desk.   The
               children are delighted.*)

NELLIE: Oh look, children – a little pigeon.

KIDS: Awww . . .

NELLIE: I have an idea. We will all go out for a nature walk in the
               fields and let the little pigeon go.

               (*They all leap up.*)

NELLIE: Wait for it . . . When I say . . . Class . . . Dis . . . MISS!

               (*Chaos and pandemonium as the kids all rush out.
               MARIAN enters.*)

MARIAN: Nurse Nellie, I've got some terrible news.

NELLIE: Don't tell me they're going to redesign the Centre again . . .

MARIAN: No. Not that. Much worse.

NELLIE: Alright dear – just calm down and tell me all about it.   Trust
               me – I'm a nurse.

MARIAN: It seems that the Sheriff has a wicked plan to get rid of the
               babes . . .

NELLIE: What?   That really nice man?

MARIAN: He's not a nice man at all.   If the babes die – or if he can . . .
               get rid of them somehow – he'll inherit all their money.

NELLIE: Goodness gracious!   But what is this wicked plan?

MARIAN: He intends to drag them into Sherwood Forest and leave
               them to the mercy of the wild Wolves that hunt in packs
               therein.

NELLIE: Wherein?

MARIAN: Therein – in the forest.

NELLIE: Let me get at him! I've a black belt in judo, a yellow belt in karate and a suspender belt in hiding. Oh! Double me gusset! What are we going to do?

MARIAN: We must get a message to Robin Hood in the heart of Sherwood Forest. He'll know what to do. The trouble is that the Sheriff's men are guarding all the ways into the woods and they'd be sure to stop us.

NELLIE: I've got an idea, dear – we'll use the pigeon – pigeon post – an e-mail pigeon!

MARIAN: Yes. We could attach a message to her leg and hope she finds Robin.

NELLIE: You write the message and I'll give the pigeon directions. (*Drawing on a piece of paper – to the PIGEON.*) Now you know Stinky Smith what keeps the sewage farm?

PIGEON: (*Nodding*) COOO . . .

NELLIE: Well, you turn sharp right by his hovel – watch out for the holly tree on the hill – very prickly on the parson's nose – bear left past the baker's – no nibbling the buns – and set your course nor' nor'west . . .

PIGEON: COOO . . .

NELLIE: Then it's straight on as the crow flies till you come to Robin Hood's oak. Once you're there, hover and say Cooo, coo, coo, cooo, coo!

PIGEON: Cooo, coo, coo, cooo, coo?

NELLIE: That's pigeon for "Special delivery for Robin Hood please sign and print your name – four groats to pay".

PIGEON: COOO . . .

MARIAN: Brilliant. Now – I'll attach the message.

NELLIE: And . . . away she goes . . . bless her little fluffy feathers.

(*The PIGEON flies off up the wire with much cooing.*)

MARIAN: Oh, Nurse Nellie – I do hope this works.

NELLIE: Of course it will, dear. Trust me, I'm a nurse. In the
               meantime, I shall not let those babes out of my sight. Not
               by day nor yet by night.

MARIAN: But look!

NELLIE: Where?

MARIAN: Here comes Fairy Tweet. She'll help us.

               (*FAIRY TWEET flies across, wings flapping, humming
               happily to herself and off.*)

NELLIE: Well! I've not never seen nothing like that in Bedminster!

MARIAN: (*Calling*) Fairy Tweet! Come back. We need your help!

               (*FAIRY TWEET flies back (backwards) and hovers.*)

TWEET: Did somebody call?

MARIAN: Fairy Tweet – you must help us.

TWEET: Tell me your troubles and I'll make them go –
               That's what Fairies are for, you know!

MARIAN: The Sheriff . . .

TWEET: What a nice man!

MARIAN: He's not a nice man.

NELLIE: He's an evil . . .

MARIAN: Beastly . . .

NELLIE: Vicious . . .

BOTH: Villain!

TWEET: Oh no he's not!

MARIAN:
NELLIE: Oh yes he is!
AUDIENCE:

MARIAN: You must believe us . . .

(LXQ.14; FSQ.5)

Trio: (*FAIRY, MARIAN, NURSE NELLIE*)

FAIRY: I WON'T LISTEN TO THIS LOAD OF BULL –
TO ME THE SHERIFF'S MR. WONDERFUL.
DON'T YOU DARE TO TRY TO PULL THE WOOL
OVER MY EYES –
HE'S JUST SO NICE!
HE'S A MAN TO MAKE A FAIRY'S HEART
FLUTTER SO IT SEEMS TO START APART.
WHEN I SEE HIM WITH THAT GIRL AND BOY
I FEEL A WHIRL OF JOY
HE'S JUST SO NICE!

MARIAN/
NELLIE: ARE YOU MAD? STOP THIS FOLLY!
HE'S AN EVIL OLD WALLY
AND HE HATES KIDS, BY GOLLY, TOO.
HE IS VILE AND HE'S VICIOUS –
FULL OF GUILE AND MALICIOUS –
THOUGH HIS SMARM HAS BEEN CHARMING YOU.
YOU MUST HELP US TO THWART HIM
TO LOCK UP AND DEPORT HIM
AND BEFORE HE CAN DO MUCH WORSE.
HE'S NOT NICE – IT'S JUST A POSE
YOU CAN'T SEE BEYOND YOUR NOSE
TRUST ME (HER), FAIRY, I'M (SHE'S) A NURSE!

(*They repeat their choruses simultaneously. FAIRY TWEET flies off in a huff at the end. Blackout.*)

(*LXQ.15; FSQ.5A; FlyQ.3) (LXQ.16*)

Scene Four

An alleyway in the poorer quarter. The SHERIFF enters DL with the PIGEON on his left wrist.

SHERIFF: Coo coo, my pet,
I'm in your debt –
There's not a pigeon faster.
She brought that note
Across the moat
And flew right to her master.
Gadzooks what guile,
I'm really vile,
They're caught hook, line and sinker.
Upon my word,
This pretty bird
Is a proper little tinker.

My feathered friend
Would never send
A fax to fetch me peril
(*Attaching a message.*)   So here's a note
What I just wrote.
Take it to Robin . . . Beryl!

(*The PIGEON flies off.*)

SHERIFF: The note will lure
                The fool I'm sure
                From his secret Sherwood grotto
                Into my trap –
                The silly sap!
                Be evil – that's my motto!
                But, in all my wickedness, I must be wary –
                So – not a word to the flamin' Fairy!

(*He goes. The old RED-HAIRED BEGGAR hobbles on.*)

SHERIFF: (*To the BEGGAR*) You poor man. (*He gives him a plastic
                spoon.*) Here's something for a cup of tea. (*He goes out
                DL.*)

(LXQ.17)

(*The BEGGAR throws off his disguise. It is ROBIN. He
blows his horn.   The MERRY MEN scramble and swing in
from all sides.*)

ROBIN: You – keep guard. (*Calling off.*)   The rest of you – spread
                out – surround the place.

FRIAR TUCK: This is too dangerous, Robin.   We shouldn't've come.

ROBIN: Me?   Miss the chance of an archery competition?   You
                saw the poster the pigeon brought.   See. (*Producing it.*)
                A contest to find the best Bowman in all England.   A
                chance to win the famous silver arrow.   I could never miss
                that.   Never.

LITTLE JOHN: But it might be a trap.   (*Snatching a "WANTED" notice
                from the wall.*) Look at this.

ROBIN: What's that, Little John?

LITTLE JOHN: The Sheriff's put a massive price on your head – a thousand
                guineas.

ROBIN: That's inflation for you. But he'll never catch me, the stupid fool. (*Throws the proclamation to another Man.*) That villain we thought was such a very nice man has turned out to be a total tyrant. How much longer are we going to allow him to get away with it? He's raising the peasants' rents – driving the poor from their homes – throwing innocent folk into the castle dungeons . . . But don't worry. I know how to deal with tyrants!

(*There is a cough off.*)

ROBIN: Quick. Someone's coming. Hide!

(*They hide. The RED-HAIRED BEGGAR enters.*)

ROBIN: (*Leaping out and seizing him*) Ah ha!

(*The disguise falls to the ground, revealing MARIAN.*)

ROBIN: Marian, it's you! Are you alright?

MARIAN: Yes. Did you get the message?

ROBIN: About the tournament?

MARIAN: No. About the babes. The Sheriff means to do away with them – but first he means to capture you. The tournament is a trap.

ROBIN: He won't catch me. I'll win the silver arrow, rescue the children and take them to safety.

MARIAN: Be careful. He's a ruthless man.

FRIAR TUCK: He'll be toothless when we're through with him . . .

ALL: Aye . . .

MARIAN: He will stop at nothing . . .

ROBIN: And neither will we – to rescue the babes.

ALL: Aye!

ROBIN: Loyal friends, take care. And remember – when you hear this horn, disband and take cover. We will meet up again in Sherwood Forest – agreed?

ALL: Agreed.

ROBIN: Are you with me, Marian?

MARIAN: Of course, Robin.

ROBIN: And you, my Merry Men – are you with me?

ALL: Aye!

ROBIN: Then on to Nottingham Castle and the tournament.

(LXQ.18; FSQ.6)

           Song: OUTLAWS BOLD (*ROBIN, MARIAN and MERRY MEN*)

ROBIN: I'M ROBIN HOOD –

MERRY MEN: AND WE'RE THE MERRY MEN.
                    WE'VE TROD THE WOOD
                    SINCE NOBODY KNOWS WHEN.
                    WE ROB THE RICH –
                    GIVE MONEY TO THE POOR
                    AND DON'T PAY COUNCIL TAXES ANYMORE

                    WE'RE FREE – WE'RE OUTLAWS BRAVE –
                    DON'T WASH WHEN WE OUGHTER –
                    GOT NO SOAP AND WATER.
                    WE LIKE TO MISBEHAVE
                    AND DO WHAT WE WANT TO DO –
                    WOULDN'T YOU?

ROBIN: (*Furtive*) I'M ROBIN HOOD –

MERRY MEN: (*Furtive*) AND WE'RE THE MERRY MEN, etc.

           (*As they tiptoe off, a FLAMBOYANT FANFARE. Blackout.*)

(LXQ.19; FSQ.6A; FlyQ.4) (LXQ.20)

Scene Five

The Tournament. A Musical Joust – Knights on hobby-horses (BABES on stick horses). A canopied stand UC. with the Lists in front of it. An

Archery Target R. Lots of banners, pennants and pageantry. NEDDY is in the stocks and the BABES are throwing sponges at him.

Fanfare.

SHERIFF: (*Over a Loudhailer*)   Good people all – I welcome ye from the city and shire of Nottingham and the surrounding settlements – to my humble castle grounds – to witness the Grand Annual Tournament and to enjoy a really good day out with fun for all the family.   For the kiddies, the Jousting Zone is to your right.   For the Mums, the Archery Zone is on the green before us – and, for the Dads – Miss Violet Culpepper – otherwise known as The Body Zone – is round the back of the refreshment tent.   Enjoy yourselves . . .

(*A cheer.   A band strikes up in the background.*)

SHERIFF: (*Approaching NELLIE and NED*)   I want a word with you two . . .

(*NED tries to sneak off.*)

SHERIFF: You too!

NELLIE: Yes, your Grace?

SHERIFF: I want you to keep an eye on the babes for me. (*He winks grotequely – WINK WINK.*)

NELLIE: An eye on the babes?   (*WINK WINK.*)

SHERIFF: Yes.   An eye on the babes. (*He winks.*)

(*NURSE NELLIE winks.   NED winks.*)

SHERIFF: Stop that.   Look at you.   I hope you're not soft hearted.

NELLIE: He's not soft hearted – just soft.   Alright – we'll keep a careful eye on them if that's what you want.

SHERIFF: I don't think you quite understand.   Come here. (*They get very close to the SHERIFF who shakes them off.*)   Now listen, scum . . .

NELLIE: Yes – Chum.

NED: Chum – my favourite! (*NED barks.*)

SHERIFF: Stop that. I want you . . .

BOTH: Yes?

SHERIFF: . . . to do . . .

BOTH: Yes yes?

SHERIFF: . . . some dirty work for me.

NELLIE: Dirty work?

SHERIFF: Yes. Dirty work.

BOTH: Ooooohhh . . . Dirty work.

SHERIFF: I am the guardian of those two miserable brats.

NED: I'd be miserable if you were guarding me.

SHERIFF: My brother's children – should anything . . . happen to them . . . I get everything. You understand? So! Dirty work is needed.

NELLIE: Dirty work?

SHERIFF: I want no bungling. They must disappear . . .

NELLIE: (*Horrified*) Disappear?

SHERIFF: . . . and you will get fifty crowns.

NED: Does that include VAT and expenses?

SHERIFF: Shut up! You've got this one chance. I am prepared to give you numbskulls wealth beyond your wildest dreams.

NED: Money?

NELLIE: Time share?

NED: A season ticket for the Rovers?

SHERIFF: Better than that.

NELLIE: Shares in Badgerline?

SHERIFF: No. Now listen. You must take them to the sinister shadows of Sherwood Forest and there – deep in the depths of the darkest dingle . . . (*He mimes slitting his throat.*) Kkkkkkkkk!

NELLIE: Not kkkkkkkkkkkk?

SHERIFF: Kkkkkkkkkk!

BOTH: Ooooooohhhhhh!

(SQ.6)

SHERIFF: Do it – and I will reward you.

NELLIE: But we can't . . .

SHERIFF: Fail me – and it's curtains.

NELLIE: Draylon or net?

NED: (*Trembling*) Curtains? Did you say . . . curtains?

NELLIE: Oh – pull yourself together.

SHERIFF: Kkkkkkkkkkkkkk!

NELLIE: But we could never . . .

NED: Not never . . .

SHERIFF: If you don't – I'll have you hung . . .

NED: We're back to the curtain gags again.

BOTH: Oooooh!

SHERIFF: Drawn . . .

BOTH: Ooooohhh!

SHERIFF: And quartered . . . !

BOTH: Oooooooohhhhhhhhh!

SHERIFF: Swear to me that what I have told you will always be . . . our secret.

BOTH: No

SHERIFF: Swear.

BOTH: Never.

SHERIFF: (*Drawing his dagger*) Swear.

NED: Bother!

NELLIE: Oooohhhh . . . Bedpan!

SHERIFF: Now swear your allegiance.   Repeat . . . after me

BOTH: After me.

SHERIFF: I hereby swear . . .

BOTH: I hereby swear.

SHERIFF: That I will do dirty deeds . . .

BOTH: That I will have dirty knees.

SHERIFF: That I will administer all that I am shown . . .

BOTH: That I will in Bedminster chew on a bone.

SHERIFF: To the best of my limited ability . . .

BOTH: To the best of my filleted mobility.

SHERIFF: To help the Sheriff to amass the cash.

BOTH: To help the Sheriff to sausage and mash.

SHERIFF: Now say Scrogglybogglyrapapapatu!

BOTH: Pardon?

SHERIFF: You heard – Scrogglybogglyrapa papa tu!

BOTH: Scrogglybogglystuck right up the flu!

SHERIFF: Nooooo – Scroggly!

BOTH: Noooooo – Scroggly!

SHERIFF:	Boggly!
BOTH:	Boggly!
SHERIFF:	Rapapapatu!
BOTH:	I'm stuck on the loo!
SHERIFF:	Noooooo. Listen carefully . . . Scroggly Boggly Rapapapatu.
SHERIFF:	Scroggly-boggly-rapapapatu!
BOTH:	Scroggly-boggly-rapapapatu!
SHERIFF:	Good! Now don't let me down.
NELLIE:	Trust me – I'm a nurse. See that wet – see that dry – cut my throat if I tell a lie . . . (*She crosses her fingers.*)
SHERIFF:	Don't forget. Tonight's the night. If you fail, I shall have you hung, drawn and quartered. (*He leaves.*)
NELLIE:	I've already been hung in the Academy, drawn in the sweep and quartered in the Bedminster Barracks.
NED:	What was that word again?
NELLIE:	Scroggly-boggly-rapapapatu!

(LXQ.21; FSQ.7)

> Song: *SCROGGLYBOGGLY RAP* (*To "Turkey in the Grass".*)
>
> WITH A SCROGGLE AND A BOGGLE
> AND A RAPAPAPATU
> YOU CAN FOOL THE SHERIFF SOMETIMES
> WITH A BOWL OF STICKY GLUE
> YOU CAN STICK IT ON HIS BOTTOM
> YOU CAN STICK IT ON HIS KNEE
> WHICH MAKES IT PRETTY TRICKY
> IF HE WANTS TO HAVE A . . .
> CUP OF TEA IS YUMMY –
> A CAN OF COKE IS TOO
> SLAP IT ON YOUR TUMMY WITH A COCK-A-DOODLE
> DOO
> BUT TANGO TIZER LILT AND COLA TOO

IS THE STUFF TO GIVE YOU WINDY POPS WHEN YOU
LEAST WANT IT TO.

(LXQ.22; FSQ.7A)

NED: What are we going to do?   What are we going to do?

NELLIE: Save the babes, of course.   It's up to us now, Neddy.
                When I give the signal, whoever's guarding them – wallop
                'em on the head.   Then we kidnap the kids and carry them
                off and conceal them.

NED: Take them to Robin?

NELLIE: We can't.   The roads are guarded – Marian told me.   We'll
                conceal them in – the castle.

NED: But that's where the Sheriff lives.

NELLIE: Exactly.   Then that's the last place he'll look.   Now
                remember – when I give the signal . . .

NED: When you give the signal . . . What is the signal?

NELLIE: When I nod my head – you hit it.

NED: When you nod your head – I hit it.

NELLIE: Right.   Oh . . . If only Robin Hood was here . . .

SHERIFF: (*Over the loudhailer*) Dear Ladies . . .

NED: (*Terrified*) Look out!   Dracula's back.

NELLIE: Act natural!

NED: (*Shaking*) This is natural . . .

SHERIFF: Dear Gentlemen – Dear Friends!

KNIGHTS/
LADIES/   (*To the AUDIENCE*)
PEASANTS/   He's such a nice man!
ROBBERS:

SHERIFF: Let us commence the Archery Contest to discover the finest
                Bowman in all England – to be winner of the Silver Arrow!
                And – the silver arrow will be presented by . . . the flower of

Nottingham City . . . the lovely . . . the delectable . . .
(*Getting carried away.*) the luscious and delicious . . .
Lady Marian.

(*Fanfare. A Cheer.*)

SHERIFF: Will the first contestant step up to the mark?

(*A PEASANT steps to the mark, takes aim at the target and fires. Another PEASANT, standing near the target falls, clutching the arrow in his chest.*)

SHERIFF: Disqualified. Go to the Boiling in Oil Zone and tell them you're next.

(*The PEASANT exits sadly. The other PEASANT is carried off.*)

SHERIFF: Next . . .

(*NEDDY steps up to the mark. He takes aim with his eyes tight shut and fires his arrow straight up in the air. He steps forward to look at the target. A rubber chicken, amid a cloud of feathers, drops out of the sky and knocks him to the ground.*)

SHERIFF: Disqualified. I shall stop that rubber chicken out of your wages. Next . . .

(*The RED-BEARDED BEGGAR steps forward.*)

SHERIFF: Curses! Who's this old bundle of rags? Where is Robin Hood?

NELLIE: (*Pulling NEDDY to his feet*) Pull yourself together. Ready for the signal?

NED: Yeh. What was the signal?

NELLIE: When I nod my head – you hit it.

NED: Ready . . .

NELLIE: Now! (*She nods her head. He hits it.*) Not me, you fool!

(*They grab the BABES while the SHERIFF is distracted and exit.*)

NELLIE: If only we could find Robin Hood . . . (*They rush off with the BABES.*)

SHERIFF: Well, get on with it, you old cesspit!

             (*The BEGGAR fires his arrow which lands in the bullseye. Fanfare. A cheer.*)

SHERIFF: I don't believe it.   You can't have the silver arrow!

MARIAN: But he won it.

BEGGAR: Fair and square, your Honour!

PEASANTS: Give him the arrow!

ALL: Yeh!

SHERIFF: Oh alright, alright.   Marian – present the arrow to the old rent-a-wreck.

MARIAN: As the finest Bowman in all England, I award you the silver arrow of destiny.

ROBIN: (*Throwing off his disguise*)   Thanks, Marian.

MARIAN: Robin!

             (*Fanfare.*)

SHERIFF: Robin Hood!   Seize him!

             (*DICKON and CEDRIC lumber forward.   MEN-AT-ARMS leap forward.   ROBIN fights them all.   Fight music.*)

ROBIN: (*Calling to MARIAN*)   Where are the babes?

MARIAN: I don't know.   They've disappeared.

SHERIFF: The babes?   Where are the babes?   (*Overdoing it.*) They've been kidnapped!   Where are my darlings?   I appeal to you . . .

ROBIN: Not to me, you don't!

MARIAN: It's no use, Robin!   Save yourself.

SHERIFF: Stop him!   Kill him!   Find the babes!

ROBIN: (*Catching hold of a banner*)   See you in Sherwood, Marian
               ...! (*He swings off.*)

SHERIFF: (*Pushing and cuffing ROBBERS and MEN-AT-ARMS*)   The
               babes, you fools – the babes!   Find the babes!

               (*Blackout.*)   **(LXQ.23;   FlyQ.5)   (LXQ.24)**

Scene Six

The same Alleyway.

*NEDDY and NURSE NELLIE enter DL, pushing a roadsweeper's cart – the
two-bin variety.*

NELLIE: It's up to us now, Neddy.   We have to keep the babes out
               of his clutches.

TOM: (*Lifting lid and popping head out*) But what's the matter?

TILLY: (*Lifting lid and popping head out*) We wanted to see the
               archery.

TOM: Yes.   Why did you rush us away, you rotten old nurse!

NELLIE: That will do.   Little children should be shaken and not
               stirred.   (*She slams the lids down on them.*)

MARIAN: (*Entering*) Quick.   The Sheriff's men are coming.   They're
               searching everywhere for the Babes.   Have you seen them?

BABES: (*Popping up*) We're here.

MARIAN: We must get them away at once . . .

NELLIE: Tell you what, You take the babes to the castle and hide
               them in my room.

MARIAN: But the Sheriff's there . . .

NELLIE: In my room?

MARIAN: At the castle . . .

NELLIE: Then he'll never think of looking there, will he?

DICKON: (*Off*) I'll check all the pubs . . . You look down that way . . .

CEDRIC: (*Off*) Yeh! I'll look down that way . . .

NED: Look out. Here they come . . .

NELLIE: Quick. Take them to the castle . . .

TILLY: Don't want to go to the castle . . .

TOM: Want to go back to the tournament . . .

NELLIE: (*Slamming the lids down on them*) . . . and keep them out of sight. We'll watch out for the Sheriff's men and keep them occupied . . .

NED: How are we going to keep those ruffians occupied, Jelly?

NELLIE: Nelly. I shall play a little game on them . . .

NED: A game? Oh golly how jolly! What do we have to do, NN?

NELLIE: You stand there and I go off and come back again. And I shall pretend to be a buzzy bee. I'll buzz around you like this – and you say to me: "Busy Bee, Busy Bee, What have you got in your hive for me?" And then you get the big surprise.

NED: I like it. I like big surprises.

NELLIE: Now can you remember the words?

NED: Yes: "Busy Bee, Busy Bee, What have you got in your hive for me?" And then I get a big surprise.

NELLIE: You're quick.

NED: My second name's Beckham.

            (*NELLIE goes off.   She immediately returns, buzzing and fluttering.*)

NED: "Busy Bee, Busy Bee, What have you got in your hive for me?"

            (*She squirts water over NED and exits laughing.*)

NED: (*To the AUDIENCE*) Charming. Am I daft? Or am I daft?

AUDIENCE:	You're daft!
NED:	Alright. Alright. Thanks a bundle.
CEDRIC:	*(Enters DL)* Ah ha! Right, you! I've had my superstitions about you all along . . .
NED:	*(Cool)* Hey . . . Cedric, my man . . .
CEDRIC:	Bog off!
NED:	Would you like a nice surprise?
CEDRIC:	Never been known to say no.
NED:	Right. Well, I go off and come back like a big bee, buzz around you and you say:"Busy Bee, Busy Bee, What have you got in your hive for me?" And then you get a big surprise.

(NEDDY goes off and returns, fluttering and buzzing.)

CEDRIC:	Busy Bee, Busy Bee. What have you got in the hive for me?

(NEDDY squirts water over CEDRIC and exits DR, laughing.)

CEDRIC:	You can go off people, you know.

(NELLIE re-enters – with a secret mouthful of water.)

CEDRIC:	Hey, Nurse Nellie. Would you like a big surprise?

(NELLIE nods "Yes".)

CEDRIC:	Right. You stand there and I go off. When I come back I shall be a busy bee. I'll buzz around and you say to me: "Busy Bee, Busy Bee, What have you got in your hive for me?" And then you get a big surprise. OK?

(NELLIE nods. He goes off, returns and buzzes around waiting for NELLIE to speak. CEDRIC grows more and more exasperated with his mouth full of water. NELLIE makes no attempt to say a thing. At last, CEDRIC swallows his water.)

CEDRIC: (*Shouts*) You're supposed to say: "Busy Bee, Busy Bee, What have you got in your hive for me?"

(*NELLIE squirts water over him. He chases her off DR. As they exit, the BEGGAR enters L. An identical BEGGAR enters R. They rush towards each other and embrace.*)

MARIAN: Robin!

ROBIN: Marian!

MARIAN: You're safe.

ROBIN: But where are the babes?

MARIAN: They're safe with Nurse Nellie at the castle.

ROBIN: We must escape to the forest and make plans to rescue them . . .

(*He blows his horn, the MERRY MEN rush, leap and swing on.*)

ROBIN: Come on, men – You two – stay here. (*Calling off.*) The rest of you surround the place. it's up to us now to see evil thwarted and virtue triumphant!

(LXQ.25; FSQ.8)

Song: OUTLAWS BOLD (*ROBIN, MARIAN, MERRY MEN*)

ROBIN: I'M ROBIN HOOD –

MERRY MEN: AND WE'RE THE MERRY MEN.
WE'VE TROD THE WOOD
SINCE NOBODY KNOWS WHEN.
WE ROB THE RICH –
GIVE MONEY TO THE POOR
AND DON'T PAY COUNCIL TAXES ANYMORE

WE'RE FREE – WE'RE OUTLAWS BRAVE –
DON'T WASH WHEN WE OUGHTER –
GOT NO SOAP AND WATER.
WE LIKE TO MISBEHAVE
AND DO WHAT WE WANT TO DO –
WOULDN'T YOU?

ROBIN: (*Furtive*) I'M ROBIN HOOD –

MERRY MEN: (*Furtive*) AND WE'RE THE MERRY MEN, etc.

              (*As they tiptoe off. Blackout.*) **(LXQ26.; FSQ.8A;
              FlyQ.6) (LXQ.27)**

Scene Seven

The Blue Chamber of the Castle.

*Door left – Bunk Beds UR against the side wall (capable of retracting into
it), a large Cupboard UL, a Grandfather Clock against the wall L. A Suit
of Armour (live) UC.*

NELLIE pushes NEDDY on in a perambulator.

(LXQ.28)

NELLIE: So this is my room . . . If only "Through the Keyhole" could
see me now.   What d'you think of it as a whole?

NED: As a hole it's fine but as a room it's awful.   Why do you
think the Sheriff put you in here?   It's ever so creepy.

NELLIE: Well, it has got a touch of the Wookey Holes. But he said
that the Blue Chamber was the nicest room in the castle . . .

NED: (*Scared*) The . . . Blue Chamber?

NELLIE: The Blue Chamber.

NED: Not . . . the Blue Chamber?

NELLIE: What's the matter with the Blue Chamber?

NED: But everybody in Nottingham knows that . . . the Blue
Chamber . . . is 'aunted.

NELLIE: Oughtn't it? Oughtn't it to what?

NED: Not oughtn't it? 'Aunted.

NELLIE: Now don't be so stupid. I don't believe in ghosts . . .

NED: Don't believe in ghosts?

NELLIE: (*Firmly*) There are no such things – as ghosts!

NED: Well I'm not sleeping here.

NELLIE: You'll do as you're told. We've got to keep an eye on the
            Babes – to make sure the Sheriff doesn't get to them before
            Robin can come to the rescue.   Once we've got them into
            bed, we'll barricade the door . . .

NED: Barricade the door?

NELLIE: Lock ourselves in . . .

NED: With the ghosts . . .

NELLIE: There are no such things – as ghosts!   We barricade the
            door so the Sheriff can't get in . . .

NED: And so we can't get out. Oh . . . Mummy!

NELLIE: Stop it. Act natural.

NED: (*Shaking all over*)   This is natural.

NELLIE: Relax. Trust me – I'm a nurse.

            (*There are noises off as the BABES approach.*)

NELLIE: Sssh! They're coming. Now don't let them see you're
            frightened. Pretend we're ready to go to sleep . . .

            (*NELLIE sticks a dummy in NED'S mouth, rocks the pram
            fiercely and sings.*)

NELLIE: GO TO SLEEP, DEAR NEDDY –
            CLOSE YOUR PRETTY EYES –
            EVEN THOUGH THEY'RE BLOODSHOT

BABES: (*Entering*) THEY LOOK LIKE TWO PORK PIES!

NELLIE: Right now you little tinkers, we'll just go and get ready for
            bed and, when we come back we expect to find you fast
            asleep. Nightie nightie.

            (*NURSE NELLIE pushes NED out in the pram.*)

BABES: Pyjama pyjama.

TILLY: There's something going on.

TOM:	I know. But what?
TILLY:	Search me. Something to do with Uncle Eustace – but Nurse Nellie and Nutty Ned aren't telling us.
TOM:	Right – let's frighten Nursey when she comes back. That'll make her tell us.
TILLY:	How can we do that?
TOM:	We need two broomsticks . . . (*Taking two from the corner.*) like these . . . and these slippers (*Fitting them onto the broomsticks.*) . . . and a sheet. This is what we do. (*They whisper.*) Now you hide in there – in the clock . . .
	(*TILLY climbs into the grandfather clock. TOM leaps into bed, under the sheet, with the "feet" sticking out. NURSE NELLIE returns.*)
NELLIE:	Well now, let's see how you're getting on . . . Good boy, Tom. But where's Tilly?
TOM:	She's in bed.
NELLIE:	She's not.
TOM:	She is.
NELLIE:	She is not.
TOM:	In that case . . . she's . . . disappeared! Been gobbled up – by the . . . ghosts!
	(*An owl hoots.*) *(SQ.7)*
NELLIE:	Course she hasn't. There are no such things as ghosts! She's just gone for a . . . gone to the . . . She's having a. .
	(*The clock strikes and frightens her.*) *(SQ.8)*
NELLIE:	Oh . . . only the clock . . .
	(*She leans against it. After several quick bongs, a canary comes out of the clock, tweeting and going mad . (SQ.9) It makes raspberry and drops a doo doo on her head.*)

NELLIE: Aaaahhh!

TOM: Nurse, I think there's something wrong.

NELLIE: What d'you mean?

               (*TOM "levitates" from the bed.*)

TOM: I feel very peculiar . . .

NELLIE: Tom!   Stop that at once.

TOM: I can't.   I'm being carried by ghostly hands . . .

NELLIE: Aaaahhh!

               (*The "body" moves around the room in pursuit of her.   She
               backs towards the clock.   The clock opens and TILLY
               comes out as a ghost under a sheet.   They both chase her
               until she grabs the sheets and discovers them.   Laughter.
               Suddenly, heavy, metallic footsteps are heard
               approaching, groans, rattling chains.   (SQ.10)   They
               freeze.*)

TOM: It sounds like . . . a suit of armour.

NELLIE: Who'd be wearing a suit of armour at this time of night . . . ?

TILLY: Nobody except . . .

NELLIE: A ghost?

TOM & TILLY: A ghost . . . !

NELLIE: There are no such things as . . .

               (*The door creaks open and a shadow is thrown across the
               room.*)

ALL: Aaahhhhh!

               (*NED enters with his feet stuck in metal buckets with a
               potty on his head.*)

NED: I got stuck in the broom cupboard below stairs!

NELLIE: It's you!

NED:	Course it's me.
NELLIE:	There you are. I knew it.
NED:	And you were quite right. *(Closing the door and barring it.)*
BOTH:	There are no such things as ghosts!

(The cupboard creaks open (SQ.11) revealing a Skeleton within. They hear it but don't see it.)

NED:	*(Tense)* D'you ever get that feeling?
NELLIE:	Not often these days.

(The door creaks shut.) (SQ.12)

NELLIE:	There are no such things as ghosts!

(The Suit of Armour steps forward, raises its visor and there is an echoey moan.) (SQ.13)

NED:	What was that?
NELLIE:	Somebody moaned.
NED:	Only the wind.
NELLIE:	I don't know what his trouble is but somebody moaned.

(NEDDY has his back to the wall L. A Spider slides down the wall and hovers just over his head.)

NELLIE:	*(Seeing the Spider)* Neddy!

(The cupboard opens (SQ.14) to reveal the Skeleton.)

NED:	*(Seeing the skeleton)* Nursie!
NELLIE:	There's a spider!
NED:	There's a very thin person!
NELLIE:	Over your head!
NED:	Behind you!

ALL: (*Running to huddle together*)   Aaaaaahhhhh!

(LXQ.29; SQ.15)

> (*Pandemonium – the Skeleton leaps out of the cupboard and dances about, the Suit of Armour marches up and down. The Bird in the grandfather clock shoots in and out with a variety of birdcalls, the Spider runs up and down the wall and the beds slide in and out – ending up out. The goodies cling together in terror. Suddenly – there is a pounding on the door.*)

(LXQ.30; SQ.16)

SHERIFF: Are – you – there?

NELLIE: The Sheriff!

GHOSTS: AAAAHHH!

> (*The Ghosts all vanish and the haunting stops.*)

NED: Oh. It's the Sheriff – what a relief.

NELLIE: A relief? He's after the babes. He mustn't get in.

SHERIFF: Are you there? Are you within?

NELLIE: No.

SHERIFF: Then I swear by the hair of my chinny-chin-chin . . . if you don't do my bidding, I'll do you in!

NELLIE: Well we won't! So there!

SHERIFF: Then let me have the babes – I know they're in there – and I'll take them into the forest myself. If you want a job doing . . .

NED: No.

NELLIE: Never.

NED: Not ever.

NELLIE: We won't let you in.

SHERIFF: Won't you? Well . . . we'll see about that . . .

(Footsteps moving off.) **(SQ.17)**

NED:　　　　He's going . . .

NELLIE:　　He's gone . . . And, in any case, we're safe.　These walls are three feet thick.　He'll never get in here!

(There is a huge "BOOM" (SQ.18) and the back wall shakes, a chunk of plaster falls off.)

TOM:　　　　Ooooh . . . I'm frightened.

TILLY:　　So am I.

(Another "BOOM".) **(SQ.19)**

NELLIE:　　Just keep calm and sing a song.

BABES:　　DID YOU EVER EVER EVER IN YOUR LONG-LEGGED LIFE SEE A LONG-LEGGED SHERIFF WITH A LONG-LEGGED
　　　　　　　　　　　　　　　　　　　　　　　　WIFE?
　　　　　　NO I NEVER NEVER NEVER IN MY LONG-LEGGED LIFE SEEN A LONG LEGGED SHERIFF WITH A LONG-LEGGED WIFE, ETC.

(NED and NURSE join in tentatively at first then more robust.　More noise from the SHERIFF.　Tractors and bulldozers are now heard.　Battering rams.　(SQ.20)　There is a huge CRASH!!) **(SQ.21)**

(And then:　(LXQ.31) The SHERIFF appears by smashing his way through the back (breakaway) wall, leaving the shape of himself as he enters.　A brick falls and knocks out NURSE NELLIE as a part of the wall hinges down and knocks out NED.　A final brick bonks the SHERIFF on the head.　He staggers but recovers.　He seizes the BABES as:)

MUSIC: FINALE

(The set begins to break apart, (LXQ.32;　FlyQ.7;　SQ.22) and truck off, transforming to:)

Scene Eight

The depths of Sherwood Forest.

ALL: THE NIGHT IS WILD
                THE BABES BEGUILED
                WHERE IS THE VILE ONE LEADING?

                WHAT DREADFUL DEED
                SPURRED ON BY GREED!
                HE WILL NOT HEED THEIR PLEADING.

                THE TEMPEST ROARS –
                THE TORRENT POURS –
                YET HE IGNORES THEIR CRYING.

(LXQ.33)

SHERIFF: WE'RE GOING TO
                A BARBECUE

                (He drags them, through fronds of gauze, into the dark forest.
                Wolves are seen and heard howling (SQ.23) against the moon.)

ALL: WE PROMISE YOU, HE'S LYING!

                HEAR THUNDER CRASH
                AND CRACK AND CLASH
                THE NIGHT LIT UP BY LIGHTNING

                BEASTS WILD AND FOUL
                THAT ROAR AND HOWL
                AND LICK THEIR JOWLS – HOW FRIGHTENING!

                BABES ARE HANDCUFFED –
                SHERIFF WELL-CHUFFED
                THOUGH A BIT PUFFED FROM THE FIGHT

                EVIL VILLAIN
                FINDS IT THRILLIN'
                TO BE KILLIN' IN THE NIGHT

                (The BABES break free and hide among the foliage.)

(LXQ.34)

                THE BABES BREAK FREE
                TURN FAST AND FLEE
                FROM TREE TO TREE IN HORROR

SHERIFF: WHAT DO I CARE?

                    SOME WOLF OR BEAR
                    WILL EAT THEM ERE TOMORROR.

ALL: SHERIFF SHAMELESS –
                    BABES ARE BLAMELESS –
                    NOW THEY'RE DAMELESS IN GREENWOOD.

                    SCARED AND WEEPING
                    WOLVES ARE CREEPING
                    SO WHAT'S KEEPING ROBIN HOOD?

                    (*NURSE NELLIE and NEDDY revive, the FAIRY (appalled
                    at the SHERIFF) flies in from DR.*)

(LXQ.35)

TWEET: DEAREST CHILDREN, DO NOT BE AFRAID –
                    ALL OUR CARE IS FOR YOU.
                    WARM AND SAFE IN SHERWOOD'S PLEASANT SHADE –
                    ON LEAFY BOWER LAID
                    AND WHILE YOU'RE SLEEPING
                    WATCH I'M KEEPING O'ER YOU . . .

                    (*During which BIRDS appear and, led by FAIRY TWEET,
                    they cover the BABES up with leaves.   Leaves are also
                    dropping from the sky.*)

(LXQ.36)

                    (*Curtain. End of Act One.*)

ACT TWO

(LXQ.37; FSQ.9)

Scene One

PROLOGUE (Before the Panto Gauze)

SHERIFF: All is mine – vast wealth untold
              Precious stones and tons of gold.
              I've diamond mines and oil wells drillin'
              So bubbles to you lot – I'm a rich old villain.

              *(Flash DR.) (PyroQ.2; LXQ.38; FSQ.10) (FAIRY TWEET
              appears.)*

TWEET: I'm feeling sick –
              Been totally tricked –
              You seemed such a pillar of virtue
              But now I see –
              It's up to me –
              To use magic spells to hurt you.
              A charm I'll put
              Around your foot
              That should stop you bragging –
              And keep you home –
              No more to roam –
              Like electronic tagging.

SHERIFF: Your spells aren't scary –
              You futile Fairy –
              You cannot do me harm
              I'm better protected
              Than you expected –
              While I wear (*Producing it from his doublet dramatically.*)
              The Sorcerer's Charm!

              (A DRAMATIC CHORD.)

TWEET: Where did you thieve it?

SHERIFF: You'd better believe it – twas left me by Mum and Dad –
              Two more festering evil ancestors no Sheriff ever had.
              When all's said and done,
              I'm the second son
              Of a witch called Morgan le Fey –

You'll admit she was quite
An evil and bright
And wicked witch in her day.
And then, God rot 'im,
Merlin Bottom
Was Dad and so your work'll
Be not worth a fig
For the Bottoms are big
In every Magic Circle.
And so, adieu –
Sucks boo to you –
The babes are now no more
And, now that I've got
Such a lovely lot,
I'm off – for a laugh at the poor.

TWEET: The babes have been rescued by Robin Hood
And are safe in his bower in Sherwood wood

SHERIFF: Babes rescued? Curses! Do the babes live yet?
But not for long, Fairy, don't you fret! (*He exits in a rage.*)

(LXQ.39; FSQ.9A)

TWEET: I must fly fast through snow and hail
To warn that the Sheriff is on their trail.

(*Birdsong.*) *(SQ.24)*

TWEET: But heark – the Lark – the Winter's past –
And Spring is bursting through at last.

(*Music. Lights come up behind the Gauze.*) *(LXQ.40)*

Scene Two

Sherwood Forest. The Forest in Winter with deep snow and icicles.

Music: TRANSFORMATION AND BALLET

(*Winter into spring. The snow vanishes from the ground and from the trees. Flowers sprout and leaves and blossoms burst out into glorious colour.*) *(LXQ.41; FlyQ.8; FSQ.10A)*
(*Spring Flower Dancers drive off JACK FROST. The Gauze Flies out.*) *(FlyQ.9; LXQ.42)*

(*The BABES are revealed among the foliage.   They look a little frightened and lost.*)

TILLY: Robin said to wait here.

TOM: But it's still pretty scary.

                (*Wolves howl.*) *(SQ.25)*

TILLY: Listen to the wolves . . .

TOM: Hello?

TILLY: Sssh. They'll hear you.

ROBIN: (*Echo*) Hello?

TILLY: I told you so . . .

(LXQ.43;   FSQ.11)

                Song: LITTLE SIR ECHO (*BABES, ROBIN, MARIAN and MERRY MEN*)

BABES: LITTLE SIR ECHO, HOW DO YOU DO?
                HELLO . . .

ALL: (*Echo*) HELLO . . .

BABES: HELLO . . .

ALL: (*Echo*) HELLO . . .

BABES: LITTLE SIR ECHO, WE'RE VERY BLUE
                HELLO . . .

ALL: (*Echo*) HELLO . . .

BABES: HELLO . . .

ALL: (*Echo*) HELLO . . .

BABES: HELLO . . .

ALL: (*Echo*) HELLO . . .

BABES: HELLO . . .

ALL: (*Echo*) HELLO . . .

BABES: WON'T YOU COME OVER AND PLAY

ALL: (*Echo*) AND PLAY

BABES: YOU'RE A NICE LITTLE FELLOW, WE KNOW BY YOUR
                                                    VOICE
                BUT YOU'RE ALWAYS SO FAR AWAY . . .

ALL: (*Echo*) AWAY . . .

                (*ROBIN, MARIAN and the MERRY MEN rush on.*)
                (*LXQ.44; FSQ.11A*)

TILLY: Robin!

TOM: Marian!

TILLY: It's you!

TOM: We're safe!

ROBIN: Now you've nothing to fear, Babes . . . The Sheriff will
                never find my hideout in the forest.   I'll keep you safe
                there until we can find some way to defeat him and reclaim
                your fortune . . .

TOM: I'd rather stay here with you and be a merry man.

TILLY: And I could be a merry woman – when I'm older.

ROBIN: Stay for now and welcome.   But remember, you are the
                rightful owners of Nottingham Castle and Tommy here will
                be the Sheriff when he grows up.   And I'm sure he'll be the
                finest, fairest, kindest sheriff any city ever had . . .

ALL: Hurray . . .

                (*Music: A Morris Dance strikes up ("The Nutting Song")
                which is joined by NURSE NELLIE and NED in full Morris
                Dance regalia.   At the end of this, ROBIN, MARIAN, the
                BABES and the MERRY MEN dance off leaving NELLIE and
                NED gasping on the floor.*)

(*LXQ.45*)

NELLIE: I can't go another step. I'd test positive for Philosan.   I'm knickered.

NED: Don't you mean knackered?

NELLIE: No. My breath's coming in short pants.

NED: Well, at least we know the way to Robin's hideout.

NELLIE: Let's check those directions that Marian gave us.

NED: (*Reading*) We came straight through the wood as far as we could . . .

NELLIE: (*Reading over his shoulder*) . . . and turned left at the glade where the red deer played . . .

NED: . . . then right at the mark in the oak tree's bark –

NELLIE: (*Wringing our her garment*) . . . leapt over the water the way we oughter . . .

NED: So now we've got to . . . "enquire of the skunk in the beech tree's trunk" – what skunk?

SKUNK: (*Popping up*) Thith thkunk. (*Farts.*)

BOTH: Phwaaaahhh!

SKUNK: I'm thorry I'm tho thmelly. (*Farts.*)

BOTH: We're thorry you're tho thmelly too . . .

NELLIE: So tell us quick – before my nose drops off – what do we do?

SKUNK: (*Farts.*)

NED: Is this going to be in code?

SKUNK: Thlide down the thlope . . .

BOTH: Thlide down the thlope . . .

SKUNK: Thlip through the thicket . . .

BOTH: . . . through the thicket . . .

SKUNK: Accroth the moth where they're playing cricket. Whithtle twithe and thout out "What-ho!" And there you'll be – in Robin Hood'th grotto. (*Farts.*)

NED: Well that thounds thimple and thtraightforward . . .

SKUNK: I don't thuppothe you'd thtay to thupper? I'm thtewing thome baked beanth and muthy peathe. (*Farts.*)

NED: Is that wise?

NELLIE: No thank you.

SKUNK: Nobody ever thtayth for thupper.

NELLIE: I'm not thurprithed.

SKUNK: Thee you thometime!

NELLIE: Anything else?

SKUNK: (*Farts and goes.*)

NELLIE: So – did you get all that?

NED: I couldn't avoid it!

NELLIE: No. The directions. Did you get the directions?

NED: (*Tapping his head*) All in here NN.

NELLIE: There's plenty of room for it. Are you sure?

NED: Trust me – I'm a nitwit. Come on.

NELLIE: I can't go another step. I shall rest here a while – in the shade of this glade – and commune with nature. You go on ahead and tell them I'm coming.

NED: But what if the Sheriff . . . ?

NELLIE: The Sheriff? If he sets foot in the forest, I'll transmogrify him with my womanly allure.

(*NEDDY falls about.*)

NELLIE: You can laugh but, when you're older you'll understand the power of transmogrification.

NED: Well come on.

NELLIE: No. You go on ahead. I shall change. (*She goes.*)

(The RED-HAIRED, BEARDED BEGGAR limps on. He drops his disguise. It is the SHERIFF.)

SHERIFF: I've prowled the woods for hours and hours
To get the sprogs back in my power.
Yet not a sign – no hair nor smidgin –
I've even lost me flamin' pigeon.
I've looked in the nook by the babbling brook and where the birds are trillin' –
Yet, without as doubt, I shall find them out. Trust me – I'm a villain!

NELLIE: (*Off – sings*) "Some enchanted evening . . ."

SHERIFF: Could be my lucky day . . .

NELLIE: "You may find a stranger . . ."

SHERIFF: And they don't come any stranger . . .

(NURSE NELLIE enters – very French.)

NELLIE: Bonjourno! Hello, big boy.

SHERIFF: Do you know who I am?

NELLIE: I sure do. Wotcher, cock.

SHERIFF: Sir, to you.

NELLIE: Sir Cock.

SHERIFF: No no, you stupid fool.

NELLIE: Oh. Naughty me. I made a boo boo.

SHERIFF: My good woman . . .

NELLIE: I'll be your bad woman if you like.

SHERIFF: I'm so glad I met you here in this leafy glade. After all, you beautiful women are just like flowers.

NELLIE: How d'you mean?

SHERIFF: You grow wild in the woods.

NELLIE: (*Simpering*) Oh. D'you think my looks are heavenly?

SHERIFF: Like nothing on earth.

NELLIE: D'you like my hair swept up?

SHERIFF: It's better than leaving it on the floor. But tell me . . . Why are you only wearing one glove? Did you lose one?

NELLIE: No – I found one. Course, I'm beautiful on the inside.

SHERIFF: Pity you weren't born inside out.

NELLIE: Did you know that I was a bubble dancer?

SHERIFF: Really?

NELLIE: Yes – but my career just . . . blew up in my face. You can imagine how I felt. I was beside myself.

SHERIFF: You must have made a repulsive couple. You begin to drive me wild, you saucy thing. Carry on like this and I could have a breakdown.

NELLIE: You know some people have got it and some people haven't got it and you've . . . got it.

SHERIFF: Yes, but I never get a chance to use it. (*Putting his hands on her shoulders.*)

NELLIE: Take your hands off.

SHERIFF: Why?

NELLIE: Any pressure makes my knicker elastic sag. Oh, Shirley!

SHERIFF: Sheriff!!!

NELLIE: Oh, Shelf-life! How you do treat a poor maiden. You turns us upside down like an old robber's dog and play with our dreams like bubbles in the air.

SHERIFF: Don't you realise that I'm passionate for ye. I've only one thing to say to you . . .

(LXQ.46; FSQ.12)

SHERIFF: (*Sings*) I'M FOREVER BLOWING BUBBLES –
                PRETTY BUBBLES IN THE AIR.

NELLIE: THEY FLY SO HIGH –
                NEARLY REACH THE SKY –

SHERIFF: THEN, LIKE MY DREAMS, THEY FADE AND DIE.

NELLIE: FORTUNE'S ALWAYS HIDING –
                I'VE LOOKED EVERYWHERE –

SHERIFF: THAT'S WHY
                I'M FOREVER BLOWING BUBBLES

NELLIE: PRETTY BUBBLES IN THE AIR.

(FSQ.12A)

SHERIFF: Be the Queen of my castle and I'll be your King –
                I'll buy you jewels and everything.
                I'll be your stallion and you'll be my filly –
                If only you'll take me to – Tommy and Tilly.

NELLIE: What? So that's your game is it? That's your plot.
                You're not a nice man and I quite forgot.
                Sir Eustace Bottom, I'm not so dumb –
                From now on I'll call you – Eustace Bum!
                Remember, girls – never let the grass grow under your feet.
                You might get nettles up your skirt. (*Goes.*)

(LXQ.47)

SHERIFF: Curse the woman – wretched nurse – how dare she call me
                                                            names?
                We'll see if she's so sparky when fleeing from the flames.
                I know that Robin and the outlaws and the babes are here
                                                            about
                So I'll burn them from their burrow, I'll simply smoke them
                                                            out –

                (*He produces a large torch from under his cloak and lights
                it with a giant Zippo.*)

(LXQ.48)

SHERIFF: There's a brisk breeze blowing through the trees and lots
of fine dry fuel
To feed the blaze for days and days.   Oh what joy to be
cruel!

(*He darts about, lighting the bushes which (flame projs) burst into flames.*)

SHERIFF: When Sherwood is ashes – and the flames have roared
I'll have the babes and my just reward!
And those merry men are just right for grillin'
So stick with the winner – and cheer the villain!

(*He roars with maniacal laughter as the flames take hold and the forest burns.*) **(LXQ.49)**

(*ROBIN and the MERRY MEN rush in with NURSE NELLIE, MARION, NEDDY and the BABES.*)

ROBIN: Quick men, set up a bucket chain . . .

FRIAR TUCK: Yeah.   Fetch water from the lake at Saggy Bottom . . .

(*The men set up a chain of buckets involving everybody except the BABES who cower downstage.   The SHERIFF seizes them.*)

SHERIFF: Together again, you horrible sprouts –
You should have know that I'd find you out.
So come this instant, you pesky infants, you and me have
got a date –
I'll soon be rid of you rotten kids – let me take you to your
fate!

(*He drags them out – un-noticed by the others who are all fighting the fire.   Trees can be heard crashing.   (SQ.26) NEDDY rescues the SKUNK from his burrow – holding him at arms length with a peg on his nose.   ROBIN sweeps MARIAN into his arms and rescues her as a huge tree trunk falls.   He and the others are still fighting the flames as Lights Fade to blackout.*)

(LXQ.50;   FlyQ.10) (Thunder.) **(SQ.27)   (LXQ.51)**

Scene Three

The outskirts of the Forest.

A sign says: "NOTTINGHAM – NOT FAR".

The thunder continues – rumbling away into the distance.   FAIRY TWEET stumps on – depressed. (FSQ.13)

TWEET: I got caught short –
                Too late to thwart –
                That villainous Eustace Bottom.
                By the time I could
                Get to the wood,
                The wretch had already got 'em.
                But still, at least,
                I beat the beast
                With a spell to bring this rain
                Without a doubt
                The flames are out
                And the Forest is safe again.
                But, oh, I'm pooped –
                My wings have drooped –
                Things couldn't've got much mouldier –
                I could take to drink –
                And I sometimes think –
                Oh, shove this for a game of soldiers!

(LXQ.52)

                Song: NOBODY LOVES A FAIRY WHEN SHE'S FORTY
                (*FAIRY TWEET*)
                NOBODY LOVES A FAIRY WHEN SHE'S FORTY
                NOBODY LOVES A FAIRY WHEN SHE'S OLD.
                SHE MAY STILL HAVE HER MAGIC POWER BUT THAT IS
                                            NOT ENOUGH.
                THEY LIKE THEIR BIT OF MAGIC FROM A YOUNGER BIT
                                            OF STUFF.
                WHEN ONCE YOUR FAIRY WINGS HAVE LOST THEIR
                                            GLITTER
                AND THE FAIRYTALES FOR YEARS YOU HAVEN'T TOLD –
                YOUR FAIRY DAYS ARE ENDING
                WHEN YOUR WAND HAS STARTED BENDING
                NO ONE LOVES A FAIRY WHEN SHE'S OLD.

                NO ONE COULD TOUCH ME AT ME SPLITS – ME SPLITS
                                            WERE ALL THE RAGE
                UNTIL ONE NIGHT THE WOODMAN LEFT HIS CHOPPER
                                            ON THE STAGE – WHAT A MESS!
                NOBODY LOVES A FAIRY WHEN SHE'S FORTY – ETC.

                (She exits sadly.)

(LXQ.53; FSQ.13A)

        (LITTLE JOHN enters furtively.)

LITTLE JOHN: *(Calling)* Come on, Fatso. Too much grub, that's your trouble. Too many doughnuts.

TUCK: *(Enters, puffing)* Don't start that again . . .

LITTLE JOHN: Right. We've fled the flames but now we must flee the forest. We have to cross . . . the Ravine!

        (DRAMATIC CHORD.)

TUCK: The ravine?

        (DRAMATIC CHORD.)

LITTLE JOHN: Yes. And the Sheriff has spies everywhere. So we need to be in disguise.

TUCK: But I can't fly?

LITTLE JOHN: Not in de skies, nitwit. In disguise. We must seem to be a part of the forest.

TUCK: I could turn over a new leaf.

LITTLE JOHN: Shut up.

TUCK: But what blends into the forest?

LITTLE JOHN: Leave it to me. I've got an idea. Walk this way . . .

        (They exit R. A DEER enters L, peeping shyly round the portal. It crosses to C, crossing its back legs and jumping up and down. It shuffles backwards to the cloth, locates a painted-on tree, and cocks its leg up. NELLIE takes off the head – she is facing backwards.)

NELLIE: Will you stop that!?

NED: *(Popping up in the hind quarters so that he is face to face with NELLIE)* I told you I wanted to go.

NELLIE: Pity you didn't want to go when my frock was on fire. And what's that niff?

NED: What niff?

               (*Fart.*)

NELLIE: That niff. Oh no – you didn't . . .

NED: I couldn't help it. It needed protection.

NELLIE: You do not enter into the close confinement of a deerskin in
               the company of your dearest chum with a skunk in your
               back pocket.

SKUNK: (*Pops up*) Thorry!

NELLIE: Tho I thould think. Get back below.

SKUNK: (*Disappearing*) Yeth thir!

NELLIE: So this is the way to Saggy Bottom. Now concentrate. We
               have got to get across – the ravine.

               (*DRAMATIC CHORD.*)

NED: Are you sure this is the place to cross – the ravine?

               (*DRAMATIC CHORD.*)

NELLIE: Well it says on the sign Deer Crossing.

               (*There is the sound of cantering hooves approaching from
               off R.*)

NELLIE: Sssshhh! Somebody's coming.

NED: What shall we do?

NELLIE: Don't forget. You're a deer.

NED: And you're a little darling.

NELLIE: Shutup. Act like a deer's bottom.

NED: But how does a deer's bottom act?

NELLIE: (*Putting on the head*) Just be yourself nobody'll notice . . .

(*NEDDY ducks back into skin and they trot across and pretend to eat leaves off the cloth. The second DEER (DEER B) enters at a trot. DEER B is very butch with foam rubber antlers which light up. DEER B trots past then stops and sniffs the air. He looks round slowly and does take on DEER A. DEER B shuffles away down stage and, unseen by DEER A, takes off his head – TUCK appears.*)

TUCK: What's that?

LITTLE JOHN: (*Appears at the rear*) It's a deer . . .

TUCK: It hasn't got any antlers.

LITTLE JOHN: That's 'cos it's a doe.

TUCK: A what?

LITTLE JOHN: You know – a (*Sings*) doe!

TUCK: (*Sings*) A doe!

BOTH: (*Sings*) A female deer.

(*TUCK carries on with the song and starts to dance.*)

LITTLE JOHN: Stop that.

TUCK: But what do we do.

LITTLE JOHN: Just act like a deer would. Act natural.

TUCK: Oh. Alright. If you're sure . . .

(*He puts the head back on and DEER B approaches DEER A, very butch, and begins a courtship ritual, sniffing DEER A'S bottom.*)

NED: (*Face appearing*) I don't think I like this.

(*DEER B does a little butch dance. DEER A does feminine, mincing dance. DEER B paws the ground and smoke comes out of its nostrils. They launch into the courtship dance with B very butch and A very coy. Ending with B charging at A. A sidesteps and B skids and falls over revealing JOHN and TUCK.*)

LITTLE JOHN: Didn't I tell you to act natural.

TUCK: That was natural – for a deer.

NELLIE: It's you!

LITTLE JOHN: Who?

NELLIE: You.

TUCK: Who're you?

NELLIE: (*Taking off the head*) Me.

TUCK/   You!
LITTLE JOHN:

NED: And me.

TUCK: What're you doing?

NED: Trying to get across – the ravine.

               (*DRAMATIC CHORD.*)

TUCK: So are we but it's hopeless.

NELLIE: No it isn't. All that's required is a soupçon of
               sophistication – a bit of nouse – what we educated folks is
               good at. Ah!

ALL: Well?

NELLIE: I've got it.

TUCK: Well keep it to yourself.

NELLIE: You. Get a log.

TUCK: A log. (*Exits, dragging JOHN in the skin and returns at
               once with a log.*)

NELLIE: You. Get a plank.

LITTLE JOHN: A plank?

NELLIE: You know – the thing you're as thick as.

LITTLE JOHN: Ah. (*Exits dragging TUCK and returns at once with a plank.*)

NELLIE: You. Fetch that big stone.

TUCK: That big stone. (*Exits dragging JOHN and returns at once with a stone.*)

NED: What we going to do now, NN?

NELLIE: We're going to be scientific. Ballistics!

LITTLE JOHN: There's no need to be rude.

NELLIE: We place the log – here. We place the plank across the log – so.

TUCK: So?

NELLIE: We place the stone here.

TUCK: Fat lot of good that is.

NELLIE: Shut up. Now the idea is – our deer stands on this end of the plank – then your deer jumps off the stone onto that end of the plank – and WHOOOSH!

LITTLE JOHN: Whooosh?

NELLIE: Whoosh! Our deer flies over the ravine to safety . . .

LITTLE JOHN: But what happens to our deer?

NELLIE: One thing at a time.

TUCK: It'll never work.

NELLIE: I'll show you. We need somebody to make a test flight . . .

(*Fart.*)

ALL: (*To NED*) Do you mind?

NED: It wasn't me!

SKUNK: (*Popping up*) Thorry!

NELLIE: Great. You can be our test pilot.

SKUNK: Tetht pilot?

NED: We're going to fly you over – the ravine.

              (*DRAMATIC CHORD.*)

NELLIE: What d'you say?

SKUNK: Oh thuper!   (*Farts.*)

NELLIE: Right thit him on the plank.

SKUNK: (*Farts.*)

TUCK: And hurry up about it.

              (*NEDDY does.*)

NED: Just a minute . . . (*He puts goggles and a Biggles helmet on the SKUNK.*)   There.

NELLIE: You two.   Up on the log.

              (*JOHN and TUCK get up onto the log.   They secretly attach the line.*)

NELLIE: I think he's ready to go.

NED: I think he's been already.

NELLIE: Are you sure you can manage this?

LITTLE JOHN: Easy as falling off a log.

NELLIE: Right.   Now jump.

              (*They jump.   The SKUNK flies off.*)

SKUNK: Wheeee . . . !

NELLIE: See.   I told you it'd work

TUCK: Right.   Here we go.

NELLIE: I beg yours!   We go first.

LITTLE JOHN: Why?

NED: It was our idea.

NELLIE: And anyway, you've had the practice.   Up on the stone.

TUCK: Oh, alright!   Come on, John.

NELLIE: Ready, Neddy?

NED: Fit and well, Nell!

NELLIE: We need a countdown.

NED: (*To the AUDIENCE*)   Will you give us a countdown?   Five
                – four – three – two – one – blast off!

LITTLE JOHN/   Geronimo!
TUCK:

                (*They jump.   The plank breaks. Blackout.*)   **(LXQ.54;
                FlyQ.11)   (LXQ.55)**

                              Scene Four

*A Lake in the Forest.   A groundrow of reeds and bullrushes marks the
downstage edge.   Willows grow round it and there is an island in the
middle.*

                Music: (*Ballet*)

                (*DANCERS as SWANS and WATER NYMPHS flit in and out
                of the water.*)

(LXQ.56)

                (*NURSE NELLIE enters in a bathing hat, robe with a
                bizarre bathing costume underneath.*)

NELLIE: So this is Clifton Zoo.   I thought I would take a little dip in
                the pool.   Us girls must stay trim.   An apple a day keeps
                the Doctor at bay.   But there's nothing like a pear to make
                him stir.   But now to . . . disrobe . . .

                Music: STRIPPER   (LXQ.57; FSQ.14)

                (*She starts to strip but is interrupted by the arrival of
                NEDDY in bathing suit, snorkel and flippers.*)

(LXQ.58; FSQ.14A)

NELLIE: What are you doing here?   It's women only between nine
                and eleven in this corporation pool so push off and no
                peeping.

NED: Oh go on, Nellie, let us stay.   I won't look, I promise.

NELLIE: Oh alright, but no giggling.

                (*She takes off her robe to reveal her outfit.   NED falls
                about.*)

NELLIE: I said no giggling.   Now.   I likes to do some aerobics
                before I swims.

                (*She turns on her portable player – aerobics music.   She
                gyrates, stretches, runs on spot, gets stuck in splits and
                collapses.   FRIAR TUCK enters.*)

NELLIE: Not another man – Ladies only.

FRIAR TUCK: But I'm a monk in holy orders.

NELLIE: Then I orders you to stop monkeying about and be wholly
                absent.

                (*The Music for the SAND DANCE comes on.*)

NELLIE: Oh – my favourite – I love something to remind me of the
                mystic east . . . Morocco!

FRIAR TUCK: Cairo . . .

NED: Skegness . . .

(LXQ.59; FSQ.15)

                (*They begin to dance – slightly at first – but end by doing
                the full Wilson, Keppel and Betty Sand Dance routine and
                off.*)

(LXQ.60; FSQ.15A)

                (*The SHERIFF appears rowing furiously on the lake with
                the BABES, bound, in the back of the boat.*)

SHERIFF: Three times I've been thwarted but now no more –
I'll dispose of the babes this time for sure.
With all this rain, it's not surprising
That the land is flooded and the water's rising.

(*He hauls them out onto the island.*)

SHERIFF: Come along my pretties, your fate awaits –
You'll get no help now from your merry mates.

(*Tying them to the tree.*)

SHERIFF: High water's due at ten past three –
And you'll be under it – wait and see!

(*He steps back into his boat.*)

SHERIFF: This time I'll triumph – no more hitches
So I'm off to Crib's Causeway to spend me riches.
The castle – the cash – they're all mine at last!

(*NELLIE and NEDDY enter in a boat rowing furiously.*)

NED: (*Heroic*) Hang on there, Sheriff baby.   Not so fast!

NELLIE: I'm with you, Neddy – Tack into the wind.

NED: Avast behind!

NELLIE: I beg your pardon.

(*They circle the SHERIFF'S boat and round the island. Their
boat gets stuck. NEDDY gets out, rolls up his trousers and
pushes off. They fight – the SHERIFF with cutlass and NEDDY
with a hinged oar – which hits NELLIE on the head.*)

(*The SHERIFF uncovers a canon in the stern of his boat. He
loads a ball, lights the fuse and pulls the lanyard. The gun
(repeater) fires marshmallows. NELLIE bats them out into the
auditorium.*)

(*The SHERIFF produces a bomb. He throws it at them – they
throw it back. It is thrown backwards and forwards. The
SHERIFF throws it off. The FAIRY flies on with the bomb and
drops it into SHERIFF'S boat. Flash. (PyroQ.3;   SQ.28)
Explosion and the boat tilts up before sliding slowly down
beneath the waves. The SHERIFF, standing at the prow, goes
down with it, saluting.*)

ALL: Hurray!

                (*ROBIN and MARION are rescuing the BABES as NEDDY and
                NURSE NELLIE scramble out and slap hands.*)

NELLIE: Trust me – I'm a nurse!

NED: Nice one Nellie!

ROBIN: And now, Tommy, you will be the new Sheriff of
                Nottingham.

TOM: Then will you and Marian leave Sherwood and come and
                live with us in Nottingham Castle.

ROBIN/   Of course we will.
MARIAN:

NED: And me!

NELLIE: And me!

ALL: Hooray!

                Music. *(LXQ.61; FSQ.16)* (*ROBIN, MARIAN, NURSE
                NELLIE, NEDDY, BABES, MERRY MEN*)

                ROBIN'S A WONDERFUL GUY
                SO BRAVE HE GAVE THAT KNAVE THE SAILOR'S
                                                    GOODBYE –
                OF ALL THE OUTLAWS HE'S THE BOLDEST BY FAR –
                ROBIN OF SHERWOOD IS A STAR!
                ROBIN'S A PRETTY COOL BLOKE –
                WHAT DO WE CARE IF THAT OLD SHERIFF IS BROKE?
                THE BABES ARE SAFE, A HAPPY ENDING IS NEAR.
                SO ALL GIVE ROBIN HOOD A CHEER!
                WE'RE FEELING GREAT!
                GOOD ON YOU, ROBIN – YOU'RE OUR VERY BEST MATE
                HE SHOOK THE SHERIFF AND HE SHOWED HIM THE GATE
                NOW IT'S THE TIME TO CELEBRATE.
                LET'S THROW A PARTY TODAY –
                FORGET YOUR HEAD AND LET YOUR HEART HAVE IT'S
                                                    WAY
                HANG THE EXPENSE BECAUSE THE SHERIFF WILL PAY
                SO JUST RELAX AND YOU'LL FEEL FINE –
                HAVING A WONDERFUL TIME!

(LXQ.62; FSQ.16A; FlyQ.12)   (LXQ.63)

Scene Five

The same Alley. (Frontcloth.)

SONGSHEET:

DID YOU EVER EVER EVER IN YOUR LONG-LEGGED LIFE
SEE A LONG-LEGGED SHERIFF WITH A LONG-LEGGED
WIFE?
NO I NEVER NEVER NEVER IN MY LONG-LEGGED LIFE
SEEN A LONG LEGGED SHERIFF WITH A LONG-LEGGED
WIFE.

(FlyQ.13; LXQ.64; FSQ.17)

Scene Six

The Great Hall of the Castle. Walkdown.

Finale: *(FULL CAST)*

ALL: HAPPY AT LAST,
                DANGER HAS PASSED, WELCOME TO MERRIMENT AND
                LAUGHTER.
                AFTER THIS MESS
                YOU ALL CAN GUESS,
                WE SHALL LIVE HAPPY EVER AFTER.
                HAPPY, HAPPY, HAPPY,
                WE'LL LIVE HAPPY EVER AFTER.
                ALWAYS BE WISE AND YOU WILL RECALL,
                PRIDE OFTEN COMES BEFORE A FALL.
                BUT AS OUR STORY NOW CONTENDS
                IT'S NEVER TOO LATE TO MAKE AMENDS.

SHERIFF: I WILL BE GOOD
                LIKE ROBIN HOOD,

NED: EVEN A SHERIFF CAN SHOW WILLIN'.

NELLIE: AND SO WE OUGHT
                TO SPARE A THOUGHT

ALL: FOR THIS RECONDITIONED VILLAIN!
                HAPPY, HAPPY, HAPPY, WE'LL LIVE HAPPY EVER AFTER.

WE HOPE YOU ALL ENJOYED THE SHOW.
TIME HAS COME FOR US TO GO.
BUT WE'LL BE WAITING, HAVE NO FEAR,
SO COME AND SEE US ALL NEXT YEAR.

(LXQ.65;   FSQ.17A)

(Curtain.)

THE END

BABES IN THE WOOD

Props list

ACT ONE

Scene One – BEFORE PANTO GAUZE.

Wand for FAIRY TWEET.

Scene Two – NOTTINGHAM MARKET.

Horn for ROBIN.
Bow and arrows for ROBIN.
Axe for NED.
Pile of wood.
Toy whip for TILLY.
Purse for OLD LADY.
Money in Purse for RICH PERSON.
Sack of wood for NED.
Quarterstaff for ROBIN.
Branch of tree – to use as quarterstaff for DICKON.
Wanted notice – "WANTED – DEAD OR ALIVE – ROBIN HOOD –
      OUTLAW. 1000 GUINEAS REWARD"– for the SHERIFF.
References for NURSE NELLIE.
Two certificates for the SHERIFF.
Child's rucksack for NED.
Teddy bear – in the rucksack.

Scene Three – THE SCHOOLROOM.

Door LC. Back wall with school drawings and pictures including Van Gogh
sunflowers, blackboard LC and an open window in the wall, right. Benches for
the PUPILS. One bench has legs at one end and the other legs just past centre.
If one person sits on the unsupported end and the other two get up, it tilts.

School Bell for NELLIE.
Exercise book for NED.
Cap for CHILD.
Note for CHILD.
Paper and Pencil on the Desk.

The PIGEON is rigged to fly down a fishing line and land on the desk. A second
line is attached to its front so that NELLIE and MARIAN only have to unhook
it (it has two hooks in line in its back) and turn it round so that it is ready to fly
off again. The paper "message" can be velcroed onto its foot. There is no cue

for the pigeon in the sound plot as we found it worked better for the "Coos" to be done live.

The Flying of FAIRY TWEET: Ideally this would be done on a tab-track – so that she can be moved on and off at the same time as up and down. She need never fly higher than six or eight feet and, if her harness is attached so that she is tilted at an angle of forty-five degrees, she can look quite heroic coming on from right and nicely comical always having to fly off backwards.

Scene Four – AN ALLEYWAY IN THE POORER QUARTER.

"WANTED" notice velcroed onto the Front-cloth.

The SHERIFF (entering DL) now has the Pigeon (or an identical substitute) on his left wrist. This means that the Pigeon's track-line is attached to his wrist and it's up to him to keep it taut while the second line pulls the bird off and upwards.

> Note for the SHERIFF to velcro onto the Pigeon's foot.
> Plastic spoon for the SHERIFF.
> Horn for ROBIN.
> Poster advertising the Archery Contest (this is apparently that
>   which was just stuck to the Pigeon's foot).

Scene Five – THE TOURNAMENT.

A canopied stand UC with the Lists in front of it. An Archery Target R. Stocks L. Lots of banners, pennants and pageantry.

> Hobbyhorses for KNIGHTS to joust (in front of the stand).
> Lances and shields for KNIGHTS.
> Stick Horses for the BABES.
> Sponges for people to throw at NED.
> Loudhailer for the SHERIFF.
> Dagger for the SHERIFF.
> Rubber (or foam) mallet for NED (he hits NELLIE with it).
> Arrow for the PEASANT to conceal against his chest and to flip up
>   and clutch when "shot".

The Archery Contest: The archery target has a spring-loaded arrow concealed in it for ROBIN's bullseye – a mousetrap with a retaining pin on the end of a piece of string (very high-tech) works well for this. The other arrows need not exist if all three bows have a length of wide elastic stretched between the haft and the bowstring. This will give the impression of an arrow when stretched and will vanish behind the bowman's hand (all are firng from L to R) as soon as the bow is lowered.

> Rubber Chicken and clump of feathers to fall from the grid.
> The Silver Arrow for MARIAN.
> Sword for ROBIN.
> Swords, Halberds, etc, for MEN AT ARMS.

Scene Six – THE SAME ALLEYWAY.

> Twin-binned Roadsweeper's cart.
> Bottles of Water off L and R.

Scene Seven – THE BLUE CHAMBER OF THE CASTLE.

Door L. Bunk Beds UR against the side wall (capable of trucking off with it). A large Cupboard UL containing an actor in black body suit with a skeleton painted on it. A Grandfather Clock against the wall L – the "body" of this needs to be big enough for TILLY to hide in it while the top contains the freaky Canary which can be as bizarre as the designer likes to make it. Whatever it looks like, it should shoot out on lazy tongues and contain some sort of squeezy container so that it will deposit a blob of something white on NELLIE'S head. A Suit of Armour – also containing an actor – stands UC.

The Back Wall: This is largely an arch filled in with "bricklaid" cardboard boxes painted to match the surrounding stonework – easy to knock over and safe enough for those who get hit in the head as it falls.

> A perambulator off L big enough to take NED.
> Huge baby's Dummy.
> Sheets on bunks – one for TILLY, one for TOMMY.
> Two broomsticks (modified to take the shoes).
> Pair of shoes or fluffy slippers – to fit on broomsticks.
> Child's Potty to fit on NED'S head.
> Two metal buckets to fit on NED'S feet.
> Huge Spider to fly in and out – apparently crawling up and down the
>   wall – nice if its eyes light up

Scene Eight – THE DEPTHS OF SHERWOOD FOREST.

> Large quantity of leaves for the BIRDS and FAIRY TWEET to cover
>   up the BABES.
> Also a large quantity in a leaf bag to flutter down from the flies.

ACT TWO

Scene One – PROLOGUE (Before the Panto Gauze).

Sorcerer's Charm – some sort of medalion – for the SHERIFF.

Scene Two – SHERWOOD FOREST

The Forest in Winter – transforming during the Ballet to – the Forest in Spring. This is a simple enough effect and can look wonderful but it's very labour-intensive. Ideally, "snow" – made from white felt or foam, cut into small pieces, medium-sized and large pieces – covers the cut-out scenery and every flat surface and is simply drawn off slowly – by hand or by fishing lines – to reveal everything green and blooming beneath. Rows of flowers can "grow up" from behind any groundrows and blossoms can hinge or pivot into view from behind the wing flats while a green and blossomed border can be revealed behind a leafless, snow-laden one, etc. The *piece de resistance* can be a complete "snow" floor-covering – made of many pieces – which, drawn off from all directions, reveals a verdant and flower-studded green floor beneath.

> Rustic Sticks and Handkerchieves for the Morris Dancers.
> Bell "gaiters" for the Morris Dancers.
> SKUNK puppet (We know there weren't any skunks in England in the
>   thirteenth century and that America hadn't even been
>   discovered yet – but it's panto).
> NELLIE and the SHERIFF may (or may not) want to blow bubbles during
> their duet.
> Torch (capable of apparently flaming) for the SHERIFF.
> Large "Zippo" lighter for the SHERIFF.
> A large quantity of Buckets – wooden buckets, plastic buckets,
>   galvanised buckets, fire buckets, popcorn buckets, seaside
>   buckets, etc.

Scene Three – THE OUTSKIRTS OF THE FOREST.

> Two Pantomime Deers – one male, one female.
> Log off L – round but with a flat side to it for stability.
> A prop Stone off L.
> A Plank off L. This breaks and has already been sawn and is dowelled
>   together for each performance to snap when jumped on.

SKUNK'S Helmet and Goggles for NED.
Fishing line off L to be attached to the SKUNK by a small snap-hook so that he can "fly" off.

Scene Four – A LAKE IN THE FOREST.

A groundrow of reeds and bullrushes marks the downstage edge.   Willows grow round it and there is an island in the middle.

Towel for NELLIE.
Portable Radio for NELLIE.

If the actors really want to go to town on the Sand Dance, then it is best to use a sand-tray.   This can be in two halves which look a little bit like folded up sunbeds – enough at any rate to justify their being brought on.

The Boats: are just the sides and seats of two tiny rowing boats on castors. They have no bottoms so that the actors can move them around easily with their feet. The oars need to be stiff but foam-covered (for hitting purposes).   The Gun in the SHERIFF'S boat (which fires marshmallows) can be built round any sort of toy (there are lots these days) which will do the job.

Cutlass for the SHERIFF.
Rope for the SHERIFF.
Bomb for the SHERIFF. This is round and looks like bombs always do in the Beano.   It needs to have a sparkler stuck in it and, as these are very difficult to light, has to be lit offstage and passed discreetly on to the SHERIFF under cover of the groundrows.

If there is a suitable trap, of course, the SHERIFF'S boat can actually sink and he can go down with it.   If not, he can capsize it and vanish underneath.

Scene Five – THE SAME ALLEY (Frontcloth).

SONGSHEET

Suggested Lighting Cues

ACT ONE

Cue	Effect
1	**(PyroQ.1)** Leafy light for FAIRY TWEET DR.
2	Light winter scene behind gauze.
3	Gauze flies out – add FOH – full stage.
4	Brighten for opening number.
5	Reduce a little to "acting light".
6	Romantic for ROBIN/MARIAN duet.
7	Return to state of LXQ.5.
8	Very dramatic for fight.
9	Very bright for NURSE NELLIE entrance.
10	Very colourful (pulsing?) for DAME/VILLAGERS song.
11	Return to state of LXQ.5.
12	Forestage for SCHOOLKIDS – distract from scene change.
13	The Schoolroom, bright day.
14	Dramatic and colourful for Trio.
15	Snap B.O.
16	Alleyway – Sinister, for SHERIFF.
17	Brighten – golden sunset – for ROBIN.
18	Very colourful for Merry Men March.
19	Snap B.O.
20	The Tournament – very bright, sunny day.
21	Very colourful (silly - pulsing?) for NELLIE/NED duet.
22	Return to state of LXQ.20.
23	Snap B.O.
24	The Alleyway – night – but bright enough for comedy.
25	Colourful for Merry Men March.
26	Fade B.O.
27	First view of the haunted bedroom – very spooky.
28	Add light for the scene to be played.
29	Pandemonium – lights flash and chase – lightning.
30	Stabilise at state of LXQ.28.
31	Blinding light through the shattered back wall.
32	Flashes of lightning, red flashes (as if explosions) as the transformation occurs.
33	Very dark and sinister in the forest.
34	Flashes of light as the BABES break away.

35   Rather nice woodland night as the FAIRY enters.
36   Lose FOH as the Curtain falls – leaving onstage tableau.

ACT TWO

37   Sinister light for the SHERIFF DL.
38   **(PyroQ.2)** Wintery light for FAIRY DR.
39   Lose DL SHERIFF light as he exits – wintery light spreads across.
40   Wintery light up behind Gauze.
41   Transform from winter into spring.
42   Complete transformation – beautiful spring day.
43   Reduce to romantic for song.
44   Return to state of LXQ.42.
45   Bright for comedy.
46   Comic romantic for NELLIE/SHERIFF duet.
47   Dark sinister day.
48   Series of small cues as the SHERIFF sets fire to different areas –
           localised flame projectors.
49   The whole forest in flames.
50   Fade B.O.
51   Gloomy day (Front Cloth).
52   Colourful for FAIRY song.
53   Bright for comedy.
54   Snap B.O.
55   The Lake - Romantic and magical for Swan Ballet – with mist if
           possible.
56   Bright day.
57   Very vivid – chasers? for very brief Striptease.
58   Return to state of LXQ.56.
59   Slow fade – as Sand Dance develops – to vivid sunset.
60   Very dramatic – with mist if possible.
61   State of LXQ.56.
62   Snap B.O.
63   Bright day – Front Cloth – Songsheet.
64   Add full stage for Walkdown and Finale.
65   Fade FOH as Curtain falls, leaving onstage tableau.

Follow Spot Plot

ACT ONE

Cue	Effect – Stage R Spot	Effect – Stage L Spot
1		FAIRY DR and follow.
2	PRINCIPALS.	
1A & 2A	Fade B.O.	Fade B.O.
3	ROBIN.	MARIAN.
3A	Fade B.O.	Fade B.O.
4	NURSE NELLIE.	NURSE NELLIE.
4A	Snap B.O.	Snap B.O.
5	NELLIE & MARIAN.	FAIRY.
5A	Snap B.O.	Snap B.O.
6	ROBIN & MEN.	MARIAN & MEN.
6A	Fade B.O.	Fade B.O.
7	NELLIE.	NED.
7A	Snap B.O.	Snap B.O.
8	ROBIN & MEN.	MARIAN & MEN.
8A	Fade B.O.	Fade B.O.

ACT TWO

Cue	Effect – Stage R Spot	Effect – Stage L Spot
9	SHERIFF DL.	
10		FAIRY D.R.
9A	Snap B.O.	
10A		Fade B.O.
11	TOMMY.	TILLY.
11A	Fade B.O. 5 secs.	Fade B.O. 5 secs.
12	NELLIE.	SHERIFF.
12A	Fade B.O. 5 secs.	Fade B.O. 5 secs.
13	FAIRY.	FAIRY.
13A	Fade to B.O.	Fade to B.O.
14	NELLIE.	NELLIE.
14A	Fade B.O.	Fade B.O.
15	NELLIE, NED, TUCK.	NELLIE, NED, TUCK.
15A	Snap B.O.	Snap B.O.
16	ROBIN & PRINCIPALS.	ROBIN & PRINCIPALS
16A	Snap B.O.	Snap B.O.
17	Follow Calls and FINALE.	Follow Calls and FINALE.
17A	Fade B.O. with CURTAIN.	Fade B.O. with CURTAIN.

Sound Cues

ACT ONE

Cue   Effect

1	Mobile Phone chirrups.
2	Mobile Phone chirrups.
3	Mobile Phone chirrups.
4	Mobile Phone chirrups.
5	Howling Wolves.
6	Howling Wolves.
7	Owl Hoots.
8	Grandfather clock chimes – off-key and sinister.
9	Same clock strikes three quick "bongs" then a canary tweets madly and blows a raspberry.
10	Slow, heavy, clanking footsteps approaching together with rattling chains (the groans can be added live).
11	A door creaks open – very exagerated sound – very Hammer horror.
12	The same effect the other way as the same door closes.
13	Echoey moan.
14	As SQ.11.
15	Pandemonium: Clock strikes, wild and cracked; variety of bird squawks; clanking footsteps, rattling bones, etc.
16	Slow, sinister, echoing pounding on the door.
17	Sinister echoing footsteps (the SHERIFF) recede.
18	Huge "Boom" as a battering ram strikes the wall.
19	As SQ.18.
20	Tractors and bulldozers approaching fast
21	Gigantic reverberating CRASH and falling masonry as back wall is shattered and collapses.
22	Clattering, collapsing masonry.
23	Howling Wolves.

ACT TWO

24	Birdsong.
25	Wolves howl.
26	Trees crashing down.
27	Crack of Thunder into rumbles.
28	Massive explosion.

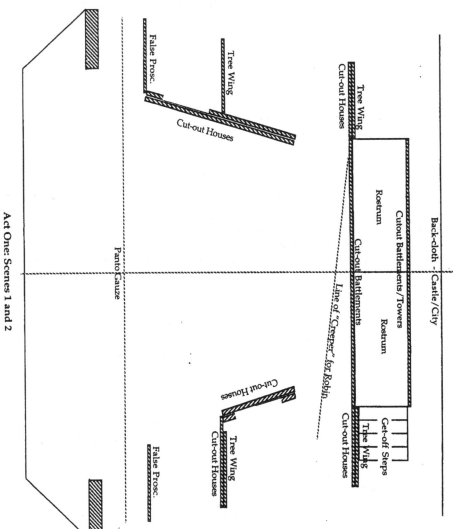

Act One: Scenes 1 and 2

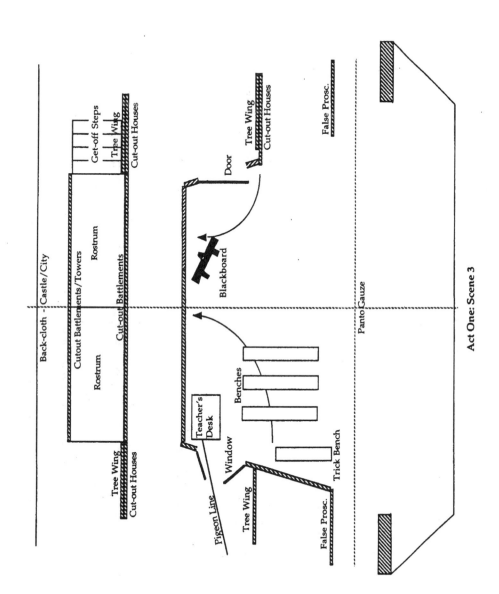

Back-cloth - Castle/City

Cutout Battlements/Towers

Get-off Steps

Rostrum

Tree Wing

Rostrum

Cut-out Houses

Cut-out Battlements

Door

Tree Wing

Cut-out Houses

Blackboard

Tree Wing

Cut-out Houses

False Prosc.

Teacher's Desk

Benches

Pigeon Line

Window

Trick Bench

Tree Wing

False Prosc.

Panto Gauze

False Prosc.

Act One: Scene 3

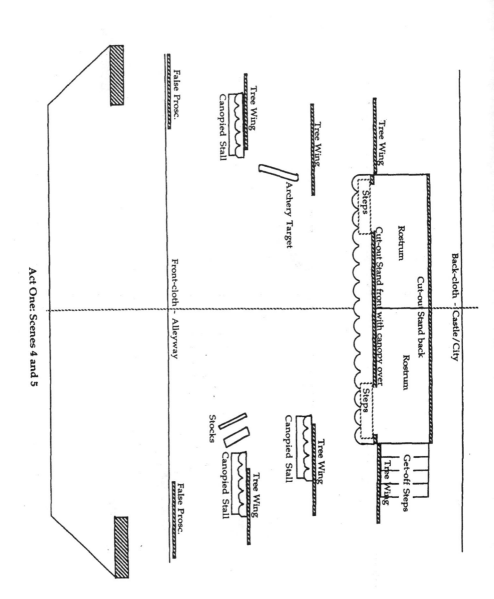

Act One: Scenes 4 and 5

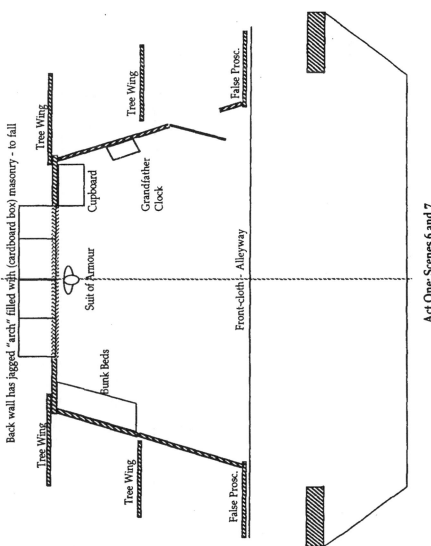

Back wall has jagged "arch" filled with (cardboard box) masonry - to fall

Tree Wing

Tree Wing

Cupboard

Grandfather Clock

Suit of Armour

False Prosc.

Front-cloth - Alleyway

Tree Wing

Bunk Beds

Tree Wing

False Prosc.

Act One: Scenes 6 and 7

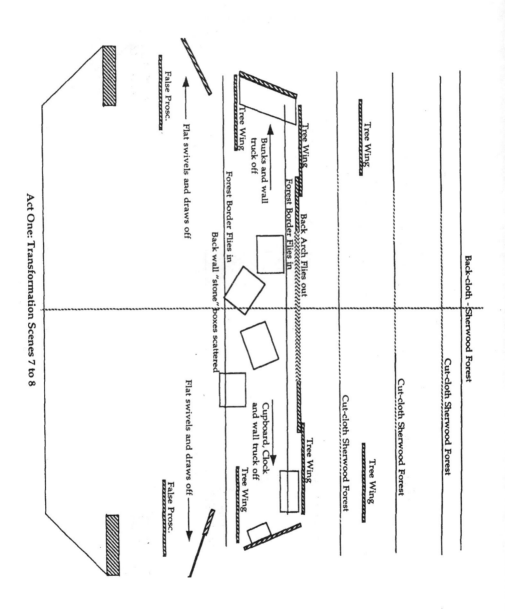

Act One: Transformation Scenes 7 to 8

Back-cloth - Sherwood Forest

Cut-cloth Sherwood Forest

Cut-cloth Sherwood Forest

Tree Wing

Cut-cloth Sherwood Forest

Tree Wing

Tree Wing

False Prosc.

Tree Wing

Tree Wing
Forest Border

Tree Wing
Forest Border

False Prosc.

Act One: Scene 8

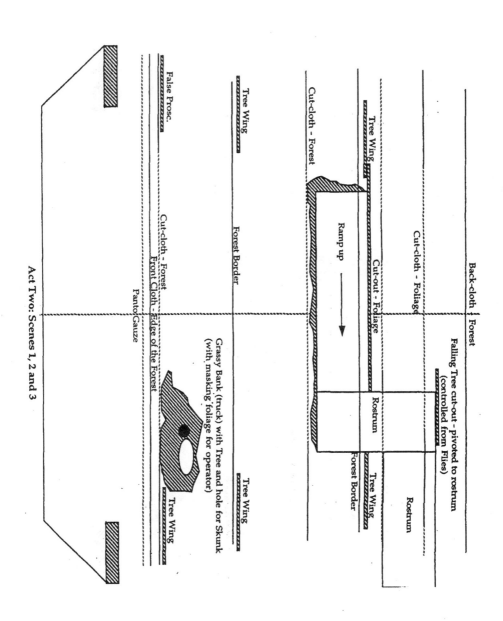

Act Two: Scenes 1, 2 and 3

Back-cloth - Forest

Falling Tree cut-out - pivoted to rostrum
(controlled from Flies)

Cut-cloth - Foliage

Rostrum

Rostrum

Forest Border

Tree Wing

Tree Wing

Cut-cloth - Forest

Cut-out - Foliage

Ramp up

Tree Wing

Tree Wing

Forest Border

Forest Border

Grassy Bank (truck) with Tree and hole for Skunk
(with masking 'foliage for operator)

Tree Wing

Tree Wing

Cut-cloth - Forest
Front Cloth - Edge of the Forest

Panto/Gauze

False Prosc.

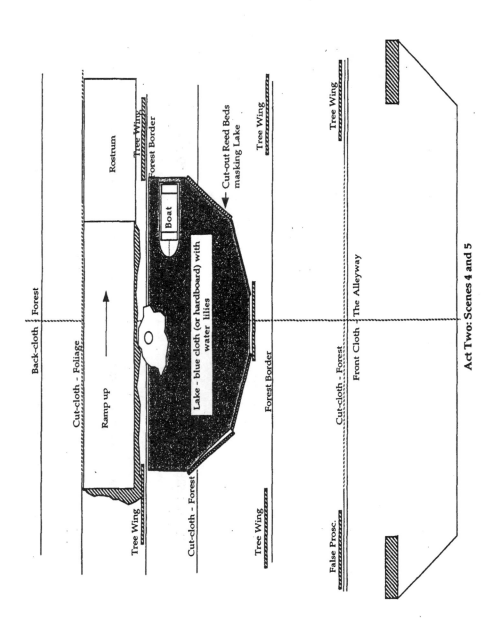

Back-cloth - Forest

Cut-cloth - Foliage

Ramp up

Rostrum

Tree Wing

Forest Border

Boat

Cut-out Reed Beds masking Lake

Tree Wing

Lake - blue cloth (or hardboard) with water lilies

Tree Wing

Forest Border

Cut-cloth - Forest

Tree Wing

Cut-cloth - Forest

Front Cloth - The Alleyway

False Prosc.

Tree Wing

Act Two: Scenes 4 and 5

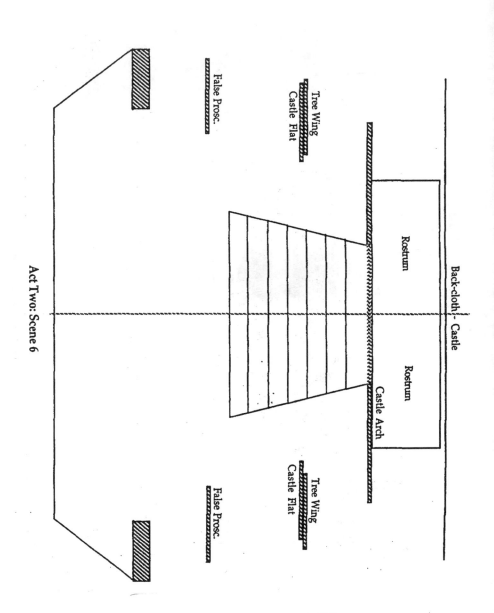

Act Two: Scene 6

False Prosc.

Tree Wing
Castle Flat

Rostrum

Back-cloth - Castle

Rostrum

Castle Arch

Tree Wing
Castle Flat

False Prosc.